W9-AFR-784

WITHDRAWN

EXPLORERS

Adventures in Courage

EXPLORERS

Adventures in Courage

By Edward F. Dolan, Jr.

Reilly & Lee Books • Chicago

105007

CODY MEMORIAL LIBRARY
SOUTHWESTERN UNIVERSITY
GEORGETOWN, TEXAS

Illustrations provided by
HISTORICAL PICTURES SERVICE • CHICAGO

Copyright © 1970 by EDWARD F. DOLAN, JR. All rights reserved.
Published by Reilly & Lee Books, a division of Henry Regnery Company
114 West Illinois Street, Chicago, Illinois 60610
LIBRARY OF CONGRESS CATALOG NUMBER 75-125375
Manufactured in the United States of America

C
910.9
D685e

This book is for Tim and Jeanie

Contents

Part One

1

New Lands

THE *Eagle,* barely missing a rock-strewn crater, had landed two hours earlier. A door in its side opened, and a man began to work his way down a ladder to the gray dust below. He moved slowly, cautiously. He wore a white pressure suit and globe-like helmet. He stood for a long moment on the lowest rung, testing the distance from the rung to the ground. Then, at 10:57 P.M. eastern daylight time, he stepped off the ladder.

His voice, sounding calm and business-like, was transmitted across 238,000 miles to more than 500,000,000 people at television sets and radios: "That's one small step for man—one giant leap for mankind."

The voice belonged to Neil Armstrong, an astronaut with America's National Aeronautics and Space Administration. The words were spoken on July 20, 1969, when, at the close of Apollo 11's three-day outbound flight, Armstrong became the first man to stand on the moon.

As the words traveled back to earth, Armstrong and all the men responsible for Apollo 11—Edwin Aldrin, Jr., just overhead in the parked *Eagle;* Michael Collins, orbiting miles above in the mother ship, *Columbia;* and the army of scientists, engineers, and technicians back at Mission Control on earth—were writing the latest and finest page in the history of exploration. It is a history that dates back to the dawn of time, a history built on man's enduring need to test his courage and to learn all there is to know of his universe, a history that has seen man venture into the most forbidding parts of his own world and at last land on the moon.

When was the history of exploration born? No one, of course, knows the precise moment, for there were no written words or cameras on hand to record it. The best we can say is that the history of exploration began thousands of years ago when our earliest ancestors gave up their forest homes and moved out to the plains. In their forests, our ancestors had survived by grabbing fruits and nuts from the trees, by scratching up roots and plants from the damp earth, and by clubbing small animals to death. But out in the harsh sunlight, they were forced to become travelers, the kind of people that all explorers must be.

Why did they travel? Because they were looking for a different kind of food than roots and plants and fruits. Somewhere along the line, they had become meat eaters—carnivores. They were now hunters of large animals.

The meat eaters' hunt kept them ever on the move, as all explorers must be. They had to seek out the water holes where the lions and the deer came to drink. They had to find the trails taken south by the caribou and the reindeer when winter was just over the horizon. They had to learn the places where the walrus and the seal gathered to breed. Theirs was a search that drove them all across the world.

In recent years, scientists have unearthed fossil deposits indicating that the first men evolved in such widely separated areas as Europe, China, India, Africa, and Java. Thanks to their hunting ways, our ancestors stalked their way to all parts of the globe, with the single exception of the frozen continent of Antarctica. Thus, our ancestors were explorers, though they would not have regarded themselves as such, insisting that they were merely searching for food. But explorers they were, for they were constantly probing into unknown lands, lands whose strangeness frightened them at first, but lands that they ultimately became familiar with. And that has always been the meaning of exploration—to advance·on the frightening unknown, learn about it, lose your fear of it, and grow to live with it.

In time, many of our ancestors turned to farming as a way of life and settled the lands that they had seen or heard about as hunters. These lands became our first centers of civilization. At least seven thousand years ago, nomads traveled down out of the Asian mountains and planted their first crops in the fertile valley between the Tigris and Euphrates rivers at the eastern end of the Mediterranean Sea. Born with that first planting was the nation called Sumer, which then developed into the mightier Babylonia and the still mightier Assyria. At about the same time, another group of people moved northward from the interior of Africa and settled along the Nile River, founding what was to become Egypt. Wanderers from the Himalayas descended through a break in the mountains to a grassy plain; there, they built Harappa, India's first civilization.

With the birth of these civilizations, exploration took a new turn. No longer did our ancestors push into the unknown in search of animal prey. They ventured forth for other reasons.

First, they sought out distant peoples so that they could trade with them, exchanging needed goods. The Sumerians broke trails into Asia Minor and India and brought back delicate fabrics and precious metals. The Persians worked their way over towering mountains to China, while the Chinese crossed the same mountains to reach Indian markets. The Phoenicians and the Minoans—whose homelands were at the eastern end of the Mediterranean—sailed out to trade with Egypt and Greece; the Phoenicians even went so far as to leave the Mediterranean and probe along the eastern and western shores of Africa. The Arabians traded at ports all along the Persian Gulf and the Red Sea.

Second, many a power-hungry ancestor of ours set out to conquer faraway countries. In about 900 B.C., the Assyrians swept out of the Tigris–Euphrates Valley, captured Syria, and then marched south to take Egypt's Upper Nile. Four hundred years later, the Persians embarked on campaigns that eventually netted them lands stretching east to India, west to the Nile, and north to central Europe. But soon the Persians fell to young Alexander of Macedon, who led his army through the wilds to such far-flung places as Turkey, the Caspian Sea, and Samarkand. Still later, the conquering armies of Rome built an empire that circled the Mediterranean and sprawled up through Spain, France, and England.

Third, at least one of our ancestors ventured into the unknown out of scientific curiosity. He was the Greek astronomer Pytheas, who, in 325 B.C., sailed out of the Mediterranean Sea and into the Atlantic Ocean. The Greeks entertained several conflicting theories on life in lands far to the north, and Pytheas wanted to replace their speculation with fact. He found his way to Britain, which he called the "Tin Islands." Wading ashore, he met the people there and saw that they wore woven clothes, ate corn, and drank a liquid called mead. It is believed that he also watched miners digging for and smelting tin ore. From Britain, he traveled farther north and, before turning back, sighted land that might have been Norway, Iceland, or one of the Shetland Islands just off the tip of Scotland.

Trader, conqueror, or scientist—they all shared traits that made them explorers. They drew charts of all the areas they visited, and they returned to tell their own peoples of the strange and wondrous sights they had seen. Thanks to their courage and their journeying, the lands around the Mediterranean—and sometimes far beyond it—became places known to early man. The world was on its way to today.

Trade, conquest, and science were not, however, the only reasons that sent early men into the unknown. Sometimes, they wanted a new life, free from strife; such was the case of the Irish monks who fled the wars of the Dark Ages and sailed north through stormy seas to discover Iceland in about A.D. 825. And, sometimes, they were wanderers by nature, as were the Vikings of Norway.

These bearded, hard-muscled men were perhaps the finest sailors that the world has ever seen. Ranging far over the northern Atlantic in their long boats, they came to the island of Iceland and made it their own in the ninth century A.D. From there, in A.D. 892, Eric the Red sailed towards the setting sun, found a great island, which he called Greenland because of the lush grass covering its western shores, and built two colonies there. In time, the climate turned so cold that ice buried the grass, with the result that the colonies fell into decay and finally disappeared altogether. But, in the meantime, Eric the Red's son—Lief Ericsson—voyaged south and sighted a new and strange coast in A.D. 1000. He called it Vinland, and we now believe it was located on the eastern shores of Canada. His discovery won him the honor of arriving in the New World almost five centuries before Christopher Columbus.

By the time of Ericsson's journey, however, a great change had taken place in most European peoples. They had turned their backs on years of trading and exploration. They made pilgrimages to distant religious shrines now and again, but their greatest wish was to remain safely at home. And they had reason to stay there, for they had fallen on bad times.

For several hundred years now, the Europeans had lived in terror. In the fifth century, Attila the Hun and his savage warriors had ridden out of their Siberian homeland and had hacked a bloody and fiery path down through Europe to the very gates of Rome. Then Mongolia's Genghis Khan and his Tartar horsemen had burned and pillaged their way through Hungary and Poland. Next, to make matters worse, the various kings and princes of Europe had taken to grabbing each other's lands, setting off a seemingly endless string of small but vicious wars. Finally, the Christian nobles had embarked on the Crusades to free the Holy City of Jerusalem from the "heathen" Turks. Numbered among their troops, unfortunately, were professional soldiers and cutthroats who did not care a hang for Jerusalem and whose only interest was in looting all the towns that lay along the way.

Is it any wonder, then, that the people of Europe built walls around their towns and castles and huddled behind them, so terrified of the outside world that they soon became fearful and suspicious of each other, of strangers, and of anyone who held beliefs contrary to their own?

Fortunately, terror was not a universal way of life. There were cities that did not seal themselves off from the rest of the world, such as Italy's Venice and Genoa. These cities traded with the countries around the Mediterranean—and even with those as far east as Arabia, Persia, and China.

Born about 1254 in one of these cities—Venice—was a man destined to breathe new life into exploration.

His name was Marco Polo.

Polo was the son of a trader who had previously traveled to China to do business with Kublai—the Khan, or Emperor, of China. When Marco was about seventeen years old, he won permission to accompany his father's trading caravan to the Khan's court at Peking. The journey eastward began in 1271, and Marco finally returned home twenty-four years later. What he had to say about all that he saw and did during those years helped to promote a new interest in exploration.

The first leg of the journey carried Marco and his father by ship across the Mediterranean from Italy to Palestine and then by camel caravan through the plains and mountains of Persia. Adventure loomed at every turn of the way for the young Venetian. One day, Marco and his father fought their way through a savage band of robbers. On another day, Marco stumbled upon a secret silver mine beneath an old castle. Time and again, he sighted Arab caravans, some of them carrying rich silk, jewels, and metalware to market, others pushing along frightened slaves for sale.

After a stop at Baghdad, the caravan pushed on to Afghanistan and climbed into the high Pamir Mountains. The air turned cold and thin, so thin that breathing and making campfires became difficult. Interesting encounters alternated with prolonged periods of loneliness. On one occasion, young Polo met a chieftain who made him a gift of several priceless rubies. But later, he and the caravan traveled for twelve days without once glimpsing another person, animal, or bird.

En route through the mountains, Marco fell desperately ill, and a year passed before he was able to climb down to the Great Gobi Desert and make his way through Mongolia to China where, one day, he sighted a cloud of dust on the horizon. The cloud evolved into a cavalry troop sent by the Khan. He had heard that the Polos were coming and had dispatched the riders to escort them the rest of the way to Peking.

The Khan welcomed his visitors to his palace of marble walls and bronze gates, shook his head with wonder at the news that they had been on the road for more than three years, and immediately struck up a friendship with Marco. He was impressed by the young man's intelligence and the fact that he had learned to speak the Tartar language like a native during his travels. The Khan was so impressed, in fact, that he urged the Polos to remain as long as possible and convinced Marco to journey to several distant areas of China as his representative on government business.

Marco visited such places as Tibet, Shansi, and Karakorum on behalf of the Khan. He was delighted and fascinated by all that he saw. He met noblemen who lived in sprawling castles, governed armies of servants, and maintained as many as thirty wives. Polo entered great cities of brightly colored buildings that bustled with commerce. He saw people using money made of paper. He saw a black rock with the ability to burn. And he saw a fibrous substance that, when mined from the earth and pressed into stiff boards, refused to burn. The first was coal and the second, asbestos.

Marco's initial journeys led to other assignments and, before he knew it, he had spent twenty years as the Khan's advisor and close friend. He was forty-one years old when he and his father finally said their farewells to the hawk-faced ruler and set out for home. In the course of the Polos' return westward, a trip of almost two years' duration, they passed through Sumatra (where they glimpsed cannibals), Ceylon, Persia, and Constantinople. They arrived in Venice in 1295, after an absence of twenty-four years.

Almost immediately, the now bearded and graying Marco began to write a book about his China adventures. A cruel disappointment awaited him at its completion. The book was distributed among the people able to read in that day and age—kings and nobles and teachers—and, to a man, they refused to believe what it had to say. They shook their heads, said it spoke of too many fantastic things, and called it wild fiction. Their disbelief haunted Marco for the rest of his days. Even when he was on his deathbed, he had to endure some friends who urged him to take back all the lies he had written. Weakly, he waved them away, saying "I have not told half of what I saw."

In time, though, the book won the respect that it deserved, for other travelers to the Orient—traders and missionaries—confirmed all that Marco had claimed to see. Now the book began to play an important role in breathing new life into exploration. It helped arouse among Europeans a fresh interest in Far Eastern lands and a mounting demand for exotic eastern goods—spices, silks, precious stones, and perfumes. And the book inspired many adventurers to find ways to fetch those goods home. They traveled out and gave what is known as "The Age of Discovery" to the history of exploration.

These adventurers, inspired by Marco Polo, knew that great wealth awaited any European who came to market with Far Eastern goods. But a trip to the Orient was risky business. The Far East could be reached only by overland routes where accidents and robber bands were many. What were needed, the would-be merchants decided, were routes eastward that promised faster and safer passage.

The obvious answer: sea routes.

The fifteenth century was dawning when the search for ocean routes to the East began. In the vanguard of the hunt was Prince Henry of Portugal, more popularly known as Henry the Navigator because of the maritime school that he established in 1416 and that developed the Portuguese into the finest sailors of the day. Believing that the Orient could be reached by sailing around the southern tip of Africa, Henry sent out one expedition after another to see if the tip itself could be reached.

Slowly, Portuguese sailors pushed their way down the western face of Africa during the next years. Captain Da Cadamosto reached the coast of Gambia (where Africa bulges) in 1455. In 1482 Diego Cam began a two-year voyage that pressed farther south to the mouth of the Congo River. A later voyage carried him to Walfish Bay, now called Walvis Bay, which lies just a few hundred miles from Africa's southern tip, the Cape of Good Hope.

Prince Henry was delighted with the rich African trade that each new southward thrust netted for his country, but he did not live to see his greatest dream come true. He died in 1460, and the Cape held off all challengers until, in 1487, Captain Bartholomew Diaz managed to put the Cape behind him. Oddly enough, Diaz did not know what he had done until days later. He had wandered about blindly in a storm for two weeks, and only when the weather cleared and he was able to get his bearings did he realize that he stood east of the Cape of Good Hope.

The next years saw such Portuguese adventurers as Vasco da Gama and Dom Francisco de Almeida sail in Diaz's wake.

They explored the eastern side of Africa and then sailed on to establish a thriving trade with seaports along the coasts of India, the Red Sea, and the Persian Gulf.

These voyages—and the trade that they brought to Portugal—were magnificent, but they paled before the accomplishment of a man who sailed into the unknown in the closing decade of the fifteenth century. He, too, was searching for a sea route to the Orient. He, too, was eager for the wealth that the trade from such a route could bring.

He did not find the route. Rather, he found a new world.

This explorer's name was Christopher Columbus.

2

Christopher Columbus

"Now TELL ME of your plan, sir."

"It is simplicity itself, Your Majesty. I wish to sail west across the Atlantic Ocean. In so doing, I expect to reach the Indies."

The man who stood before Queen Isabella of Spain in 1486 was tall, powerfully built, and of a fair and freckled complexion. His hair was red, and his eyes blue. Pride held his shoulders high. His name was Christopher Columbus.

The monarch, enthroned with her husband, Ferdinand, at their court in Cordova, heard the elegantly dressed men and women all about her gasp with astonishment at the words. But she herself remained silent. Ever since this sharp-nosed seaman had arrived in Spain a year earlier, many tales of his grandiose scheme had reached her. The time for surprise was long past.

"It is a daring plan," she said. "Except for the coastal waters about Europe and Africa, the Atlantic is an uncharted sea. There are those among us who believe it to be the home of evil monsters. Others say that it drops off the edge of the world."

Columbus held up a large hand, but the scorn that he felt for such ideas did not show in the gesture. He dared not annoy this woman. He needed her help, not her anger.

"They are mere superstitions," he said. "Surely Your Majesty has heard of what today's finest scientists and scholars are saying."

Isabella smiled. She was well aware of the most modern theories. "That our world is not flat, but a globe."

"There is much evidence to support their belief," Columbus said. He flicked his still upraised hand toward the west. "Just a few miles into the Atlantic from here lie the Canary and Azorean Islands. We know for a fact that the people of the Canaries have seen bits of timber come floating in from the west. And we also know that the people of the Azorean Islands have found the drowned bodies of brown-skinned men washed up on their western shores—men with the features of Asians."

Columbus stepped forward, his blue eyes flashing.

"All these things had to come from *somewhere*. There can be but one answer. The Indies!"

"And you wish from me the funds to sail there?" asked Isabella.

"Indeed!" replied Columbus.

Long ago, his desire to appear dignified had made Columbus slow of speech. But now his voice raced with enthusiasm. "Grant me the money to sail west," he pleaded, "while all the others still press along the old eastward routes. I shall find the Indies and give Spain a new, undreamed-of trade route to their riches."

At the end of his recital, Isabella sat back thoughtfully, and Columbus held his breath. He had spent years on the plan for his voyage. All his dreams and ambitions were bound up in it.

At last, the queen stirred. "Your proposal is an interesting one—fascinating, in fact. But the voyage promises to be expensive. Very expensive. And dangerous. You might well be going to your death . . ."

"I am willing to take that risk," Columbus persisted.

Isabella waved him to silence. "Nevertheless, you ask for a decision that I cannot—will not—trust myself to make alone. I shall need help. I must speak with my advisors and hear what they recommend."

Columbus opened his mouth to protest, to argue that the dangers involved and the money spent were nothing when compared to the riches that could come of the voyage. But he held his tongue. Isabella, he knew, was an intelligent woman. She would give his plan a fair hearing. He would just have to be patient.

But how long could he be patient? How long would it be before the queen, busy with other affairs of state, spoke with her advisors? How long before they returned a recommendation? Patient! It seemed to him that he had been patient all his life.

That life had begun at about mid-century in Genoa, Italy, where Christopher's father had eked out a living as a wool carder. Born to poverty, Columbus had received little early education, but he had been blessed with a good brain and a fine imagination. He had little interest in his father's wish to train him for the weaver's trade. Columbus wanted instead to go to sea and find great wealth.

And to sea he did go—as a boy aboard a fishing vessel and later as an able-bodied seaman on a Genoese trading ship. Then, when Columbus was in his twenties, he settled in Portugal. That country, thanks to the rich African trade resulting from its quest for the Cape of Good Hope, had become the leading maritime power of the day. In Portugal, Columbus thought, a young man with ambition and a love of the sea would find the opportunity to make something of himself.

The Portuguese years were busy ones for Columbus. He began his career as an apprentice to a Lisbon cartographer but soon launched his own chartmaking business. He married Felipa Moniz de Perestrello, the daughter of a noted sea captain. In his spare hours, Columbus studied geometry and astronomy, at the same time becoming fascinated with the theory that the world was really a globe.

All the while, he hungered for wealth and honor, and suddenly he saw that the theory held the key to both. Men still pressed eastward to reach Asian markets. Columbus would take advantage of the round-world theory and do the exact opposite. He would voyage west to the Indies, establishing a new trade route. The route would bring him wealth—and everlasting honor.

Columbus called his planned voyage "The Enterprise for the Indies," and soon the thought of it consumed his whole being. But the voyage would require money, more money than he had ever seen. He must seek out the man who could put all the resources of Portugal behind him— King John II.

Columbus won an interview with the king in 1484. John listened to him with interest—such interest, indeed, that he seemed ready to dip into his treasury at any moment. But then the royal advisors stepped forward, frowning, and Columbus heard for the first time all the arguments that would plague him for years to come. Only death awaited a man in the uncharted Atlantic—death when he sailed off the edge of the world, death when the jaws of some horrible

Christopher Columbus

monster clamped down on him, death when a giant whirlpool caught his ships and smashed them to bits. The voyage was nonsense, the scheme of a madman.

The advisors' arguments won the day, and John sent a bitterly disappointed Columbus home. The disappointment turned to cold fury weeks later when Columbus learned that the king, suspecting there might be something to the voyage after all, had secretly dispatched a ship west into the Atlantic. Its frightened crew had quickly turned the ship back.

John's treachery might well have reduced an ordinary man to a lifetime of grumbling about his mistreatment. But Columbus was no ordinary man—and he knew it. John had turned him down. John was stupid. A wiser monarch would have to be found.

And so, after months of describing his proposed voyage to anyone who would listen, Columbus stood in the court of Spain's Isabella, wondering how long he would have to wait for her answer.

That answer was slow, painfully slow, in coming. Five years passed while Isabella's advisors—and then a special commission that she appointed—haggled over the voyage. All the old, superstitious arguments were heard time and again. But at last there was agreement. The voyage might well be the plan of a madman, but it should be attempted. The riches that it could bring to Spain, if successful, made Columbus's plan worth the gamble.

Columbus heard the verdict from the queen herself in the early summer of 1492. But if Isabella had expected a show of gratitude in return, she was due for a surprise. The time had come for Columbus to talk of the wealth and honor he expected for himself from the voyage. He had been kept waiting for years and had been called a madman once too often, so his terms were to be hard ones. He drew himself to his full height. Spain, he said, was to give him the title of Admiral of the Ocean over all seas on which he sailed and was to name him governor of any new lands that he discovered during his voyage. And, further, he was to be granted 10 percent of any trade that resulted from his discoveries. Would Isabella agree? Columbus waited. She would.

Immediately, Isabella launched preparations for the long-dreamed-of voyage by making Columbus a gift of two ships. Both were caravels—small, broad-beamed, latten-rigged vessels. One was the *Pinta,* of about fifty tons. The other was the *Nina,* of about forty tons. The queen obtained the caravels from the Pinzons, a family of shipowners at the little Spanish port of Palos.

Columbus then secured a larger ship, the *Santa Maria.* It was a three-master with a cargo capacity of 100 tons, and Columbus designated the *Santa Maria* as his flagship. He assigned the *Nina* and *Pinta* to the command of two Pinzon brothers who were as eager as he to make the voyage.

While the ships, so small and frail looking, were being readied for sea duty, Columbus and the Pinzon brothers went in search of crews, a job that proved almost as difficult as any Columbus had ever undertaken. Not a sailor in Palos or any nearby village had a taste for challenging the Atlantic. The sailors were poor, superstitious fellows, and they could envision nothing for themselves on the Atlantic but death. They spread their hands, lifted their eyes, and asked, "Then, senor, who will take care of our families when we are at the bottom of the sea?"

Kings and queens had not stopped Columbus before, and he told himself that mere peasant sailors would not stop him now. He told Isabella that he would settle for any men, even criminals. She responded by proclaiming that any man in prison would be pardoned if he agreed to join the voyage. Immediately, eighty-eight volunteers spoke up—all of them inmates of the jail at Palos. Columbus signed fifty-two of their number aboard the *Santa Maria*. Eighteen each went to the *Nina* and the *Pinta*.

On Friday, August 3, 1492, almost three months after Isabella had given her permission for the voyage, the three little ships lumbered out of Palos and, unfurling sail as they went, headed into the Atlantic. The ships moved steadily through known waters to the Canary Islands, where they stopped in early September to take on additional water and stores. By September 6, they were underway again. Three days later, Columbus watched the Canaries slip over the horizon. He and his men were alone on an uncharted sea.

No sooner were the Canaries out of sight than Columbus sensed the first stirrings of fear in his crews. The men had been at ease in known waters. Now they began to think of the unknown dangers that lay ahead and to wonder if they would ever see their homes again. Columbus knew that their anxieties would increase the farther they got from Spain. And anxiety, once out of control, could mean disaster.

To keep the men's spirits bolstered, Columbus turned to subterfuge. He began to keep two logs of each day's run. One remained always locked in his cabin; it noted the actual number of miles traveled. Columbus posted the other for the crews, always making certain that it showed a lesser number of miles traveled. With satisfaction, he daily watched the men smile at the thought that they were still closer to home than they had guessed.

For the ten sailing days between September 9 and 18, the weather aided Columbus's efforts to keep fears at rest. The little fleet, with the *Pinta* always racing ahead, was caught in the easterly trade winds and was swinging along under brilliant, sunny skies. Columbus wrote that the ocean was "a delight" to see each morning. The men, happy to be free of prison life, shared their captain's delight, fishing over the sides and even plunging into the sea for brief swims. The ships were traveling so close together that the crews could easily talk across the water to each other. There were no bunks aboard the vessels—only Columbus and the Pinzons had cabins—and at night the sailors stretched out anywhere to sleep. Columbus stood on the high poop of the *Santa Maria* each evening and listened to the sailors' talk as they bedded down. They spoke quietly, joked, and sang songs of home. Columbus smiled. All seemed well—even though, by September 18, Europe lay more than a thousand miles beyond the stern.

But then, overnight, the Atlantic turned against the intruders. Beginning on September 19, the winds changed about and held, cold and fierce, from the northwest for ten long days. The men lifted faces gone pale to cloud-swept, gray skies. They muttered to each other in an anger born of sudden fear. How in heaven's name, they asked, would they ever be able to work their way back against these winds when the time came to return home? Perhaps it was best to venture no farther, to turn back right now—before things got worse. Columbus held his breath.

The winds, however, shifted round to the east before the sailors' mutterings turned into open demands to retreat eastward. The men relaxed again, but only momentarily. For then the fleet sailed into what is known as the Sargasso Sea, a stretch of the Atlantic clogged with heavy seaweed. The crews gasped in horror as the green, slimy seaweed closed round the ships, crowding up to their hulls and clinging to the wet wood. Some of the men feared that the seaweed would halt forward progress and hold them prisoners there for the rest of their lives. Others predicted that horrible monsters would soon rise out of the green slime and devour the ships. Columbus saw one man after another drop to his knees, weeping.

But a few days later—on September 23—all was miraculously changed. The Sargasso Sea was now safely astern, and every heart aboard was beating wildly. A signal had come from Captain Martin Pinzon aboard the *Pinta,* which was running in the lead, as usual. He had sighted land! It lay directly ahead, in the setting sun.

The sailors crowded along the rails and climbed to the rigging, all staring westward, all chattering excitedly. There it was! Low on the horizon! Columbus himself knelt for a prayer of thanks and then ordered all hands to sing "Gloria in Excelsis Deo." The little ships aimed their prows directly at the distant coast. The sun fell beneath the horizon, and night closed over the sea. Hardly a man slept. Everyone wanted to be looking west when the new day arrived.

But the dawn brought only bitter disappointment. The sea lay vast and empty. There was no trace of land. The men cried out in anger and frustration. They had been fooled. They realized that they had mistaken a cloud bank for land.

In their disappointment, the sailors became sullen. Their mood worsened as September changed into October. Old fears returned afresh. The men knew that they had to be at least two thousand miles from Spain, and they were more certain than ever that they would never see their homes again. They were just as certain that they should have seen land by now if, indeed, there was any land at all in the vast sea upon which they sailed.

They had come far enough, the crew said. They were on a fool's mission. They should turn for home, immediately.

105007 **CODY MEMORIAL LIBRARY**
SOUTHWESTERN UNIVERSITY
GEORGETOWN, TEXAS

And if the Captain General—as they called Columbus—got in their way, he should be tossed overboard. Even Captain Martin Pinzon aboard the *Pinta* agreed with them.

Mutiny seemed imminent, but it never came to pass. The opening days of October brought with them sights that evaporated all anger, sights that indicated land must be nearby. Seaweed and tree branches floated into view. Flights of birds wheeled overhead. Then the *Pinta*'s men fished up a long pole. It bore unmistakable signs of having been cut by human hands. As night fell on October 11, Columbus ordered all hands to keep a sharp lookout and promised a reward to the first man to sight land.

No one slept that night. All eyes peered westward. At 10 P.M., Columbus motioned a seaman named Pedro Guttierez to his side. His voice was low and tense.

"Look ahead. I thought I saw a light just then, far in the distance," whispered Columbus.

"A light, Captain General?"

"Yes. It looked like a little wax candle rising and falling."

Guttierez squinted into the night. Suddenly, his fingers gripped Columbus's arm. Yes, yes! He saw it! There it was! Just barely visible! Like a tiny candle!

Word of the mysterious light spread through the ship and then streaked across the water to the *Nina* and the *Pinta*. Sailors rushed to the bows of the ships and clambered high into the rigging. Most of the men saw only a dim view of the dark horizon. But there were some who yelled that they could see, now and again, some sort of pale flickering. After a time, the light disappeared, never to show itself again.

To this day, the light remains a mystery. Many historians have tried to guess what it might have been. Their conjectures have ranged from its being the reflection of land on the sea to a burning native torch. One—Professor Samuel

Eliot Morison of the United States—believes that it was simply an optical illusion, caused by the great desire to see land.

The night deepened, with all hands tense and the three ships plunging ahead under full sail. The water was rough and choppy—another sign that land lay somewhere nearby. Midnight came and went. Then it was two o'clock in the morning of October 12, 1492, an hour in which the whole story of mankind was to be changed.

It was then that a seaman named Rodrigo de Triano, riding high above the *Pinta*'s deck, shouted: "Land! Land!"

The words echoed across the water to Columbus, and, for a moment, he dared not believe what he had heard. All about him was the sound of rushing feet as the crewmen again dashed to the bows. Then they were shouting and pointing ahead and pounding each other on the back. Triumphant voices erupted from the *Nina* and the *Pinta*. At last, Columbus saw what everyone else was seeing—not a flickering light this time, not a cloud, but a whitish stretch of coastline looming on the horizon and glistening in the moonlight. Columbus murmured a prayer of thanks, shouted his congratulations across to the *Pinta*, and ordered the ships to drop anchor for the rest of the night. After years of waiting, he had his goal within reach. Columbus slept.

At dawn, a large island lay in the distance. Columbus viewed it silently, his back erect with pride. He felt certain that he had come to one of the islands on the outskirts of the Indies. Perhaps the Indies themselves would be found in just a few miles more. He had no idea—not even in his wildest imaginings—that he stood on the threshold of a vast new world.

With the first light of day, the three ships moved in close

to the island. A ship's boat went over the side, and Columbus, accompanied by the Pinzon brothers, rode in it up to a sandy beach. Columbus carried the Spanish royal banner, while the Pinzons held flags emblazoned with green crosses and the initials of Ferdinand and Isabella. Columbus stepped ashore. The sand underfoot was white and smooth, the surf behind him, gentle. Palm trees stood some yards inland, rustling in a soft wind. Gathering the Pinzons and the other members of his party around him, Columbus gave thanks for a safe Atlantic passage and claimed the island for Spain, naming it San Salvador.

We now know that the island lay in the Bahama group, just off the southeastern coast of North America.

At first, Columbus thought the beach to be deserted. But minutes after his arrival, brown-skinned and dark-haired natives began to assemble, coming slowly, cautiously, shyly out from the palm trees. Columbus stared. He had never seen such people before. Bartolome de Las Casas, a missionary who wrote an account of the voyage, had this to say of the natives:

> They go as naked as when their mothers bore them, and so do the women, although I did not see more than one young girl. All I saw were youths, none more than thirty years of age. They were very well made, with very handsome bodies, and very good countenances. Their hair is short and coarse, almost like the hairs of a horse's tail. . . . They paint themselves black, and they are the color of the Canarians, neither black nor white. Some paint themselves white, others red, and others of what color they find.

The natives, so painted and carrying long spears, seemed a fearsome lot at first. But Columbus sensed that they were simply curious and friendly. He stepped forward and held out several red cloth caps as gifts. These offerings were no more than simple little trinkets, but they delighted the natives. Columbus laughed at their childlike pleasure and, because he thought he was so near the Indies, gave them the name Indians.

Soon, the natives dragged long dugout canoes down to the surf. With as many as fifty men to a dugout, they paddled out to the ships and climbed over the rails. Instantly, laughter and shouting broke out everywhere. The sailors pressed beads, bits of cloth, and knives into brown hands. Into their own outstretched hands came animal hides, brightly plumaged parrots, and spears with fish-bone tips.

Columbus remained at San Salvador until Sunday, October 14, when he again set sail, his eyes ever searching the horizon for his first glimpse of the Indies. He swept past numerous tiny islands and entered the vast expanse of water that is the Caribbean Sea. A giant land mass fell across his bow on October 28, and Columbus's heart leapt with the certainty that he had reached his final destination. He ordered the ships into a large bay. Fern- and tree-covered shores coasted by to either side. Only the sounds of birds reached the ears of Columbus and his crew. Not a sign of human life could be seen. Columbus had hoped for a busy Indian port. The journey was not yet over.

Today, we know that Columbus had reached the island of Cuba and had entered a quiet bay there.

Despite the silence of the island's shores, there was human life there—brown-skinned natives who fled in terror as soon as Columbus came up on the beach. He followed them and managed to convince them that he intended no harm.

Columbus noted immediately that the Indians wore ornaments of gold—bracelets, necklaces, and anklets. After much arm–waving and pointing, he determined that the gold came from somewhere in the interior of the island. He dispatched a troop of seamen inland, their eyes glittering with dreams of treasure. They spent long days trudging over hills, poking along streams, and peering beneath tropical foliage, only to return empty-handed. But the men reported one astonishing sight. They had encountered natives who held a burning plant, rolled up, in their mouths and breathed in the smoke. Europeans and tobacco had at last met.

After remaining at anchor in his quiet bay for several weeks, Columbus voyaged along the Cuban coast. He explored its shores, visited its native villages, and—in vain—cast a sharp eye about for gold. In December, his ships headed for a large island looming to the southeast. He called it Hispaniola. Today, it is divided into Haiti and the Dominican Republic.

Columbus had performed a miracle of seamanship. He had brought three tiny ships and eighty-eight men all the way across the Atlantic without the loss of a ship or a single life. That fine record—at least, in part—was ruined on Christmas Eve, as Columbus neared Hispaniola.

The seaman at the *Santa Maria*'s helm was responsible for the trouble. Toward midnight, when Columbus and the rest of the crew were asleep, the helmsman grew so weary that he could not keep his eyes open. Contrary to standing orders, he handed the tiller to a cabin boy and threw himself to the deck. Immediately, he began to snore.

But moments later, he was wide awake, staring with alarm —as was every other man aboard—for, in quick succession, a grinding thunder erupted from beneath the *Santa Maria*, she tilted far over, and then stopped dead still, no longer rising and falling with the sea swells. In his cabin below deck,

Columbus threw himself from his bunk. He dashed top-side, knowing without a word from anyone that somehow his ship had gone aground. Then he saw *why*. A shivering boy stood at the helm; water ran swiftly just beyond the stern; the surf crashed nearby. Inexperienced in steering, the youngster had unwittingly allowed a strong current to catch the *Santa Maria* and sweep her onto a sandbar just off the Hispaniola coast.

A furious Columbus hurried below to check damages. Relieved, he saw that the vessel had not had the bottom ripped out of her and, in fact, had not even sprung a minor leak. But climbing down to the sandbar, he snorted with fresh anger. The keel of the *Santa Maria* was bedded deep in the soft sand. Much work would have to be done to free the ship—if, indeed, it was destined to be freed at all.

Much work *was* done, but all of it to no avail. The crewmen sent all provisions overside to waiting hands on the sandbar; following them came water casks, lanterns, the anchor chain, cooking ware, and even personal gear. Every pound that came overboard failed to lighten the *Santa Maria* to the point where it could float to freedom. The ship refused to budge. It was stuck in the middle of an uncharted sea for the rest of its days.

Columbus stared out at the *Nina* and the *Pinta* hovering nearby. As if the loss of his flagship wasn't enough, he now faced another problem. He had a crew of fifty-two men on his hands, plus all their provisions. By no stretch of the imagination could he hope to crowd them all into the two little ships. There just was not enough room.

Only one solution was possible. Most of the *Santa Maria*'s crew must be left on Hispaniola while Columbus, temporarily abandoning the search for the Indies, returned to Spain to fetch rescue vessels. Forty-four sailors agreed to

remain behind. They built a small fort and provisioned it
with a year's supply of food, water, and ammunition. They
christened it La Navidad—in honor of the eve of the Nativity,
when their ship had run aground. By the time Columbus
disappeared east, the sailors were comfortably settled and
were befriending the island natives.

Columbus, now aboard the *Nina,* set his course for Spain
on January 16, 1493, and entered the harbor at Palos on
March 15. At the end of a voyage that had lasted seven
months and twelve days, he stepped ashore to a hero's welcome. Church bells rang and artillery thundered. Countless
people, commoners and noblemen alike, thronged the dock
to gape at all the curios Columbus had brought home, chief
among them ten muscular—and very bewildered—brown–
skinned natives.

The explorer, feted every step of the way, traveled to
Barcelona, where Ferdinand and Isabella were holding
court. Head thrown back almost arrogantly, Columbus
was delighted to see the monarchs put all other business
aside and give their full attention to his presence. How
things had changed! No longer did he have to wait for their
words. Now they waited for his. Slowly, pausing now and
again while the monarchs and their courtiers gasped, Columbus told them of his adventures and of his certainty that the
Indies lurked just beyond the islands he had discovered.
Then he paraded before them the wonders he had brought
home—the Indians, spears, knives, wildly plumaged birds,
strange plants, and native trinkets of gold. He watched the
eyes of all fasten hungrily on those trinkets.

Now the dreams that Columbus had dreamed of wealth
and honor began to come true. Ferdinand and Isabella
named him viceroy of all the lands he had found and con-

ferred on him the title of Don, saying that he was henceforward to be treated as a Spanish grandee. They ordered a magnificent coat of arms made for him. And they told him that they wanted him to venture west again—to colonize the islands he had discovered, to find new islands, to find the source of the native gold, to rescue the men on Hispaniola, and, of course, to reach the Indies.

Columbus sailed on September 24, 1493. But now he went in style—not at the head of three tiny ships, but in command of fourteen caravels, three giant galleons, and fifteen hundred seamen, soldiers, colonists, and missionaries. The voyage netted him the discoveries of the Virgin Islands and the islands of Antigua, San Martin, Santa Cruz, Puerto Rico, and Jamaica. On Hispaniola, Columbus and his colonists founded the first Spanish settlement in the New World, calling it Isabella. Inland, he came upon a native gold mine, captured it, and began extracting its riches for Spain. But of La Navidad he found little trace. It had been reduced to ashes.

From nearby Indians Columbus learned of the disaster that had visited the fort. Its forty-four inhabitants, so friendly at first, had turned out to be intolerable neighbors, demanding free food and water and even making slaves of several natives. Finally, enough had been enough. The Indians had attacked the fort, slaughtered its defenders, and burned it to the ground.

The news of La Navidad was not the only unfortunate aspect of the voyage of 1493. The settlement at Isabella did not prosper; its colonists were spending more time hunting for gold than planting crops and were falling ill from lack of food and with the fevers of an unhealthy climate. Word of the conditions at the settlement reached Spain and

Columbus was much criticized. But far worse, in his mind, was the fact that all his voyaging west from Hispaniola won him not a single glimpse of the Indies.

Columbus returned to Spain and then made two more westward voyages, one in 1498 and a final venture in 1503. On that last voyage, Columbus sailed farther west than ever before, reaching the eastern coast of what is now known as Central America. He was certain now that he had come to the Indies, but, for all his searching along the coast, Columbus could find no busy trading centers. He sailed home, frustrated, angry, and bewildered. Later explorations by other men proved that he had been thousands of miles from his destination and that, on the far side of Central America, there loomed another ocean quite as large as the Atlantic.

The voyage of 1503 marked the end of his sailing days. Columbus was broken in health from the rigors of his explorations. He was bitter over his failure to find the Indies —and hurt when his appeals for additional voyages west were refused at court. No one was now interested in a western route to the Indies, for the Portuguese had succeeded in rounding Africa's Cape of Good Hope and had established an eastern route to Oriental markets. The route was working quite well, and everyone was content with it. So far as the west was concerned, Spain was only interested in colonization and gold-hunting. Columbus was now a forgotten man. All the honor that he had desired and won slowly slipped from his grasp.

Until the end of his days, Columbus was certain that the Indies lay just to the west of his discoveries. He had no idea that the giant land masses of North and South America sprawled to either side of the seas through which he had sailed. The discovery of those lands remained for other men, among them a man who was inspired by Columbus's voyage.

Third voyage of Columbus, 1498

This man later ventured out on his own and found Honduras, the coast of Brazil, and the Gulf of Mexico. His name was Amerigo Vespucci, and the vast lands that Columbus had sailed between were named for him.

In time, Columbus even lost the honor of being known as the discoverer of the New World. It is now known that the Vikings of Norway, under Lief Ericcson, visited the shores of what is now Nova Scotia some five hundred years before Columbus's birth. And, John Cabot—a Venetian sailing under the British flag—reached the same place at about the time Columbus was making his fourth and final voyage far to the south.

But no matter that Columbus did not touch on the coasts of either North or South America, or that the New World is not named in his honor. Word of his discoveries spread through Europe like wildfire, and one expedition after another was sent westward in the next years. Slowly but surely, following the trail that Columbus had blazed, these expeditions unveiled the vast lands of the New World.

For, leading the way, Columbus changed the course of history.

Part Two

3

A New World

Columbus, grand though his discoveries were, failed to prove the theory that the world was round. Rather, he simply demonstrated that land lay far across the Atlantic. To prove the theory, someone still had to reach the Orient by sailing west from Europe.

That job fell to the proud Ferdinand Magellan, a Portuguese nobleman working for the Spanish crown. On September 20, 1519, commanding five ships, Magellan put to sea from Seville and charted a course southwest toward South America. By this time, almost two decades after Columbus's fourth and final voyage, Spanish captains had charted much of South America's eastern face, and one of their number, Vasco Nunez de Balboa, had explored inland from the east coast of what is now the Isthmus of Panama and had glimpsed a vast ocean stretching away from its far side.

Magellan intended to probe farther south than any captain before him. In so doing, he hoped to find the southernmost shores of South America or a westward-running waterway at some point that would carry him all the way across the continent. Either would lead him into Balboa's sea. Then, if indeed the world was round, a voyage across that sea should bring Magellan at last to the Orient.

He came up to the Brazilian coast of South America in November of the year 1519. All through the next months, Magellan nosed southward, entering various bays and rivers to see if they would grant him passage through to Balboa's ocean. At last, on October 21, 1520, Magellan arrived at the southern tip of the continent and found a strait running west between it and a clutter of rocky pinnacles and islands just off shore.

Immediately, Magellan headed into the strait, which now bears his name and whose 360-mile length gave him the worst thirty-eight days of his life. Violent winds battered him every inch of the way. The cold air chilled his men to the bone and stiffened their fingers so that they could hardly work the sails and rigging. At times, the strait so narrowed that the ships barely escaped crashing into the looming rocks. The sea, pitching insanely, threw tons of water inboard to fill the holds and soak all provisions and send the men sprawling helplessly against the bulwarks. Strange and frightening fires dotted a barren coastline to the south; the crews named it Tierra del Fuego, meaning Land of Fire. They muttered that the Devil himself must live there, not knowing that they were simply seeing the campfires of an Indian tribe. As for Magellan, he wondered if the coastline might mark the beginning of a great southern land mass. Later explorations revealed Tierra del Fuego to be an island of moderate size.

The fleet broke out of the strait on November 28 and entered Balboa's sea, finding it so calm and its winds so gentle that Magellan called it the Pacific. He shaped his course northwest and traveled for ninety-eight days, passing

Guam and finally coming to the Philippine Islands. Despite the tranquil beauty of the sea and sky, the Pacific voyage was a nightmare for Magellan and his crews. Their food supply was low, and what there was of it had long ago rotted. They were reduced to eating sawdust and ships' rats to stay alive.

Magellan landed at the harbor of Cebu, provisioned his ships with food and water, and claimed the Philippines for Spain. Obviously frightened of his muskets and cannon, the natives there agreed to the claim. But the fiercely independent tribe on the island of Mactan was not so easily persuaded to surrender. Haughty as ever, Magellan armed sixty of his men and set out to bring the little island under his control.

He anticipated nothing more than a quick and simple slaughter. And for a time, the events of the day lived up to Magellan's expectations. Spanish muskets cut the islanders down with a terrible efficiency, and torches dissolved their bamboo homes into bonfires. But the islanders, blindly furious and determined to fight to the last man, refused to surrender. Massing together, they hurled themselves at the attackers, raining poison darts into the Spanish ranks. Now Magellan saw his own men begin to drop, their faces twisted in agony as the poison ate into their blood.

Terrified, the Spaniards fell into a wild retreat. Magellan dashed after them and commanded every man to stand his ground. Then, with the words barely out of his mouth, an expression of horror crossed his face, and he dropped abruptly to his knees. He looked down to see a poison dart in his thigh, then up to see his men running away and brown bodies and savage faces surrounding him. Island swords blotted out the sun and came hurtling down on him. Magellan pitched forward on his face. Seconds later, he was dead.

Leaderless, the remainder of Magellan's troops fled back

to Cebu, only to encounter fresh horrors. The natives there, no longer afraid of muskets and cannon now that they had seen what poison darts could do, called for the death of every Spaniard in sight. They murdered two officers in an alley and attacked crewmen at a beach encampment. The frightened and exhausted Spaniards took to their ships and put the Philippines behind them for good.

After all the months of hardship, the Spaniards wanted nothing more than the comforts of home, but they elected not to make an eastward return. Rather, with signs all about that the Indies were near, they pushed on west. They saw the wisdom of their choice in the next weeks when, shouting despite their exhaustion, they came into known waters, waters that had been explored earlier by Portuguese captains sailing east around Africa. They docked at India for a time and then cut a path across the Indian Ocean to Africa, finally rounding the Cape of Good Hope and beating their way up the Atlantic to a mid-1523 docking at Spain. For the first time in history, at a cost of all but eighteen lives in the expedition, the world had been circled.

Though he did not live to tell about it, Magellan had succeeded magnificently where Columbus had failed. He had found a westward trade route to the Orient and had proved that the world was actually a globe. The latter feat caused men to discard all their old ideas of geography and to see their earth through fresh eyes. People everywhere shook their heads in wonder. Theirs, they said, was a remarkable age indeed. Just thirty years ago, Columbus had given them a New World. Now Magellan had changed the shape of the whole earth.

Columbus's New World had lured one adventurer after another westward during those thirty years. Pressing deep into the Caribbean Sea and the Gulf of Mexico, explorers had branched out in three directions—north, south, and directly west—and had encountered great land masses. The mapping, exploration, and settlement of South America, Central America, Mexico, and North America had begun.

Between 1498 and 1520, Spanish captains charted most of the eastern face of South America. Then, following Magellan's sea trail into the Pacific, they probed the western side of the continent, with Francisco Pizarro conquering Peru in 1533, Diego de Almagro exploring Chile in 1535, and Jimenez de Quesada mapping Colombia in 1537. Settlers traveled with these and other explorers. Building towns, trading posts, and farms, they started the great southern continent of the New World on its way to becoming today's South America.

The mapping of Central America began when Columbus toured its eastern coast during his 1503 voyage, the fourth and last one he made to the New World. Ten years later, Vasco Nunez de Balboa landed at the Isthmus of Panama, marched inland, and stopped on a mountain peak, his breath taken away as he beheld for the first time the great ocean that Magellan later christened the Pacific. Then, in 1519, Hernando Cortez came ashore far to the north and turned Mexico into a Spanish possession, slaughtering countless Aztec Indians in the process.

Parts of North America began to fall under Spanish control on Easter Sunday, 1513, when Ponce de Leon, exploring north from Puerto Rico, came upon a sun-drenched shore and called it Florida, the Spanish name for "Flowery Easter." He was followed in 1539 by Hernando de Soto, who explored inland beyond the Mississippi. A year later—and some two thousand miles to the west—Francisco de Coronado marched out of Mexico to find a string of rich cities said by the Indians to lie far to the north. He hiked through what is

now the southwestern United States and became the first
European to see the Colorado River and the Grand Canyon.
But rich cities? He saw not a one—only wretchedly poor
Indian villages.

Spain was not the only nation of the day interested in
North America. The sprawling continent also beckoned to
England and France. In fact, England's explorer John Cabot
arrived in North America sixteen years ahead of Ponce de
Leon.

Cabot approached the New World for the first time in
1497. He anchored just off Labrador and then, with his son
Sebastian, spent the next year voyaging as far south as the
Carolinas. Thanks to that journey, England laid claim to
the eastern face of the continent down to Spain's Florida
and began to settle the territory in the late 1500s. At about
the same time, England was given a look at the distant West
Coast when Sir Francis Drake, during a trip around the
world, traveled up the coast of California in 1579. England
did not, however, press any claim to the West Coast, and
California was eventually settled by the Spanish.

Jacques Cartier launched the French exploration of
North America. Starting in 1534, he investigated the Gulf
of St. Lawrence and the St. Lawrence River as far as
the future site of the city of Montreal. French settlers arrived in 1608 and founded the city of Quebec. French explorers moved south in the next years. Father Jacques
Marquette and fur trapper Louis Joliet traced the Mississippi down to its juncture with the Arkansas River. Rene
La Salle went even farther, coasting along the great river
to its mouth at the Gulf of Mexico. He claimed the land all
around the Mississippi for France and named it in honor of
his king, Louis XIV.

From these beginnings, the colonization of eastern North

America evolved, with Spanish settlements in Florida, English ones all along the coast north from there, and French ones inland in Canada and far south at the mouth of the Mississippi. By the time of the American Revolutionary War in 1775, the colonists were several million strong, and many of the settlements had grown into cities. That war turned one part of North America into a new nation—the United States.

Among the men who helped found the new nation was young, sandy-haired Thomas Jefferson. With the end of the Revolutionary War, he looked west and felt a great dream take hold of him. Jefferson dreamed of the day when the United States would not be confined to the east side of the Mississippi but would sweep magnificently all the way from coast to coast, taking in thousands of square miles of unexplored country.

He knew that the great Missouri River flowed in from the West to join the Mississippi at the settlement of St. Louis. But from where in the West did it come? Perhaps all the way from the Pacific Ocean?

That river should be explored, Jefferson told himself. If it runs all the way to the Pacific, it could one day serve the United States as a great trade highway. And, no matter where it runs, it could carry settlers westward to give the nation new farms and cities. Also, he said, the lands all around the river should be explored. Jefferson wanted to learn about the soil of that land, its crops, its natural resources, its Indian tribes, and its wildlife. Such knowledge would be invaluable to future settlers.

But Jefferson dared not even mention such an exploration. For the Missouri ran through the vast Louisiana Territory—885,000 square miles spreading west through the heart of the continent from all along the length of the Mississippi.

The territory was owned by the French, and already their trappers were there and bringing back fine furs to market. The young United States, Jefferson knew, could not go nosing through another nation's territory. That would only invite trouble of the worst sort.

But Jefferson could not dismiss the idea of the exploration. It tickled his imagination right up to the time that he became third president of the United States in 1801. As soon as he took office, Jefferson looked west again. American settlers were moving in that direction in ever-increasing numbers. One day nothing would stop them from crossing the Mississippi and striking out toward the distant West Coast.

He made his decision. French or no French, the Missouri had to be explored, just as Canada had been explored all across its breadth to the Pacific eight years earlier by Sir Alexander Mackenzie.

As president, Jefferson would authorize an expedition into the Louisiana Territory.

4

Lewis and Clark

So far as President Jefferson was concerned, secrecy was the byword for the expedition. The whole enterprise had to be conducted in *absolute* secrecy. If any word of it reached the French, Jefferson would have an enraged Napoleon on his hands, a Napoleon who would, correctly, accuse the United States of snooping around Louisiana with the idea of one day making the region its own. The United States, as yet, was too young and small to invite the wrath of mighty France and its warlike chief.

In 1801, Jefferson began casting about for a man to head the expedition, knowing that he required someone with two talents. First, the fellow must be able to keep his mouth shut during all the months of preparation. Second, he must be a born leader, for, once on the trail, he would be taking his expedition through about eight thousand miles of wild and uncharted country, inhabited by possibly hostile Indians. Jefferson found his man in his own personal secretary—Meriwether Lewis.

Lewis, in 1801, was twenty-six years old, the eldest son of

a Virginia family long acquainted with Jefferson. Born at Charlottesville, Lewis had joined the army at twenty and had advanced to the rank of captain. Just prior to becoming the president's secretary, he had served as paymaster with the First United States Infantry, a job that took him through the wilds of the Ohio frontier to pay the soldiers garrisoned there. Lewis was a dark-haired man, gruff in manner, reserved in speech, and, in Jefferson's estimation, completely trustworthy.

But he was neither an experienced explorer nor a scientist, and so he had to be trained quickly for the job ahead. Jefferson sent Lewis to Pennsylvania friends, all of them pledged to secrecy, for his training. From them, Lewis learned the many crafts that would serve him well on the expedition—navigation, to guide his boats; medicine, to care for his men; map making, to chart the regions through which he passed; and natural science, to help him identify, select, and care for all the plant and insect specimens that Jefferson wanted brought back for study.

By mid-1803, Lewis was ready for the West. But he now felt that he would like to share with another man the great responsibility of leading the expedition, and he suggested the name of his longtime friend William Clark. Clark, born in Caroline County, Virginia, in 1770, was the youngest brother of George Rogers Clark, the Revolutionary War hero, and had served in the army with Lewis. He was an experienced woodsman and a strong leader, Lewis said. Jefferson agreed with the selection.

To some, the choice may have seemed an odd one, for the red-haired Clark was Lewis's exact opposite in several respects. Lewis was reserved, but Clark was outgoing, comfortable in any man's company. Lewis was gruff, and Clark was jovial and easy of speech. But they were to prove to be

William Clark

Meriwether Lewis

ideal companions, sharing the leadership of the expedition
and traveling for months in the wilderness without an argument or a word of dissent between them.

Soon after Clark accepted its co-leadership, the expedition
no longer needed to be kept secret. Napoleon's wars were
going badly for him, and he desperately needed money to
finance his armies. Jefferson, quick to see that the situation
could be turned to the advantage of the United States,
stepped forward. He offered Napoleon $15 million for the
885,000 square miles that were Louisiana. Reluctantly,
Napoleon nodded his agreement. Overnight, the United
States more than doubled itself in size. Now the expedition
would be traveling through American territory.

Lewis and Clark received their final instructions from
Jefferson in the autumn of 1803. Quietly, the president re-
peated all that he had told Lewis when first planning the
expedition. Travel along the great Missouri River from
St. Louis. Map its course and see whether it reaches the
Pacific. Chart the lands all about the Missouri and the rivers
branching out from it. Note the animal and plant life seen.
Bring back plants, foods, and insects for study. Make friends
with the Indians along the way and study their customs. Do
not antagonize them, and do not go off looking for personal
treasure as explorers elsewhere have done. Remember, you
are not out for personal gain. Yours is a scientific mission
for the future benefit of the whole nation.

The explorers heard the instructions through and then
were on their way. They traveled west, set up headquarters
near St. Louis, and spent the winter of 1803 in making their
final preparations. With Lewis and Clark were forty-five
men. Numbered among the men were regular army soldiers, volunteer soldiers from Kentucky, Frenchmen who
were experienced riverboat handlers, and a French-Indian

woodsman who was a crack rifle shot and an expert in Indian sign language. Most were under thirty years of age, and the youngest member of the party, George Shannon, had just turned seventeen.

Lewis and Clark began the long journey on a rainy May 14, 1804, sailing from St. Louis up the Mississippi River for a few miles and turning west into the Missouri River for a stop at nearby St. Charles. From there, in the words of their journal, Lewis and Clark "hoisted Sail and Set out in high Spirits for the Western Expedition" at 3:30 in the afternoon of May 21. Under their command were two dugout canoes, called pirogues, and a fifty-five-foot keelboat. The pirogues, one painted red and the other white, carried seven and six oarsmen, respectively. Twenty oarsmen and a sail amidships gave the keelboat motive power. Lewis and Clark rode in the keelboat, which carried a small cabin aft and swivel cannons in the bow and the stern.

The first leg of the journey took the explorers westward across Missouri to the border of what is now Kansas, then northward between the present states of Nebraska and Iowa, and through South Dakota to Mandan, North Dakota. The river was wide all along the way, and the journey was a delight to the eye.

The weather was spring-warm, with blossoms budding along the banks, and the sunny days were punctuated now and again by dazzling but short-lived electrical storms. For the first miles, much boat traffic crowded the river, as the canoes, pirogues, and rafts of French and Yankee trappers hurried their fur cargoes to the busy St. Louis markets. Game abounded on all sides, and there was no problem keeping the expedition well provisioned.

The game seemed to grow in quantity and variety as the Missouri ended its westward run near Kansas and turned to climb steadily northwest across the plains of America's Middle West. The expedition's log reported that "immense herds" of deer were constantly sighted along the shores, as were antelope, elk, ducks, turkeys, bear, and buffalo, the latter often traveling in herds several thousand strong. The whole region appeared to be a hunter's paradise. Into the log went the word that the expedition daily supped on "4 deer, an Elk and a deer, or one buffaloe." Lewis commented that a handful of good riflemen could easily keep a regiment supplied with food.

One animal, caught by a member of the expedition, was a stranger to the travelers. Clark tried his best to describe it, writing, "This Anamale Burrows in the Ground and feeds on Flesh, (meaning Prairie Dogs) Bugs & Vigatables his Shape & Size is like that of a Beaver, his head mouth &c. is like a Dogs with Short Ears, his Tail and Hair like that of a Ground Hog."

The "anamale" in question was the badger. It was hitherto unknown in America, although it was a longtime resident of Europe.

As the expedition moved north, one Indian tribe after another swept into view—first the Oto and Omaha tribes of Nebraska and Iowa, then the Yankton Sioux of Iowa, the Teton Sioux of South Dakota, and finally the Arikara, also of the Dakotas. Lewis and Clark were surprised to find the Arikara, unlike their tepee-dwelling Sioux neighbors, living in mud huts and tending lush fields of beans, squash, corn, and tobacco.

In the main, the two explorers fared well with the various tribes. They attended ceremonial dances in their honor and ate Indian-cooked food. They exchanged gifts, once receiving four hundred pounds of buffalo meat as a present. Lewis and Clark handed little medals from President Jefferson to chiefs along the way. One morning, they met with six Oto chiefs on a high bluff overlooking the river and told them that a new government, the United States, had taken over the Louisiana Territory. The chiefs smiled, conveyed their best wishes to President Jefferson, and said that they were eager to trade with the whites. The explorers christened the meeting site "Councile Bluffs." It became a central spot for conducting Indian-American affairs in the next years. It now stands about twenty-five miles from the city of Council Bluffs, Iowa.

Only the Teton Sioux gave Lewis and Clark trouble. On one occasion, a band of painted warriors stole a horse from one of the expedition's hunters, forcing him to walk the several miles back to the boats. On another occasion, as a pirogue was coming up to the shore, three braves grabbed its mooring cable and would not let it go. The explorers guessed, correctly, that the Tetons were fearful of letting the strangers enter and pass through their country. They met with the chiefs, exchanged gifts, and were allowed to go on their way. Upon the explorers' departure, a chief named Black Buffalo came aboard the keelboat and said that he would accompany the expedition for a time to protect it against other Tetons upriver. Black Buffalo bustled ashore two days later when the boat hit a log and almost capsized. He stopped long enough to say that the expedition was now safely out of Teton country.

In the midst of all these adventures, Lewis and Clark got on with the day-by-day work of the expedition. They charted all the rivers and streams flowing into the Missouri. They collected plant and food specimens and carefully stored them aboard the keelboat. Lewis analyzed the mineral content of the land, with Clark noting that his friend found one area so rich in alum, copper, and cobalt that he "was Near

poisoning himself by the fumes & tast of the Cobalt. . . .
Copperas & alum is verry pisen." Both Lewis and Clark
made many notes on the animal life they encountered, and
they bottled dozens of small insects. Once they came upon
the skeleton of what appeared to be a forty-five-foot-long
fish. They took a few of its bones away with them. Later
examination of the bones showed that the "fish" was actually
a prehistoric dinosaur.

The explorers reached Mandan, North Dakota, on November 2, 1804, marking the end of the first leg of their
journey. They had been on the move for five and a half
months and had traveled sixteen hundred miles. Gratefully,
they settled down for the winter among the Minnetaree and
Mandan Indians.

Both tribes proved to be friendly, and the winter, severe
though it was, passed quickly and pleasantly. The Indians
shared their food with the explorers and told them what
they could expect as they traveled west. They would en-
counter high mountains, the Indians said, and several rivers
flowing into the Missouri. More than likely, there would be
confusion over which river to follow. If so, the explorers
could identify the Missouri by a magnificent series of waterfalls at one point along its course. Lewis and Clark were
grateful for the information. Previous to their arrival at
Mandan, they had been helped by some old maps and by
the advice of French trappers who knew the river. But once
Mandan was behind them, they would be in completely
strange country.

The Indians also warned them to be on the lookout for
the giant and ferocious grizzly bear. The explorers had
never seen the animal and they thought the Indians were
exaggerating their descriptions of its size. Later events
caused the explorers to change their minds. First, they came

Lewis and Clark meet the Mandans

upon a grizzly track that measured seven and one-half inches wide by eleven inches long. Then they met one of the towering creatures face to face. He charged and did not drop until eight bullets had been pumped into him.

The explorers moved west on the next leg of their journey in early April, 1805. Their number was now swelled by three, for traveling with the party was a French trapper named Touissant Charbonneau, his seventeen-year-old Indian wife, Sacajawea, and their infant son, Pompey. Sacajawea, a Shoshone Indian, had been taken from her tribe as a child and had been raised among the Minnetarees.

Eager to get back to her own people and knowing that Lewis and Clark were heading into Shoshone country, she begged them to allow her to accompany them. They agreed, seeing an advantage to having her along. She could serve as both guide and interpreter. And the presence of a woman would help convince the Shoshone that the white strangers were on a peaceful mission.

Sacajawea, a cheerful and indomitable young woman, proved invaluable to the expedition. She served not only as guide and interpreter but also as cook, hunter, and nurse. Her courage inspired the men during some of the most hazardous weeks of the journey, and her good spirits heartened them daily. Clark nicknamed her "Janey" and her son "Pomp."

Because the Missouri was no longer wide and smooth but narrowing and swift as it flowed out of the rising mountains, the explorers left their keelboat behind and traveled in the pirogues and Indian dugout canoes. They paddled by the mouths of what are now the Knife, Little Missouri, and Yellowstone rivers. Then, days later, after entering what is now the state of Montana, they came to a fork in the Missouri, with one arm angling off to the northwest and the other falling away southwest. Which arm should they follow? Which one was the continuation of the Missouri?

They chose the southwest arm, naming the other branch the Milk River because its waters reminded them of the color of tea mixed with milk. Lewis and four men scouted ahead of the main party. Lewis remembered what the Mandans and Minnetarees had told him: find the great waterfalls and you will know that you are on the right track. Suddenly, he heard a deep, unending thunder in the distance. He hurried forward, then stopped to gape in wonder.

There were the falls—and what falls they were. Sometimes three hundred yards wide from bank to bank, they consisted of a series of falls, cascades, and rapids that covered a span of ten miles, staircasing the river downward some four hundred feet. The tallest of the lot was more than ninety feet high. Water fell from it in a solid sheet, only to shatter into millions of sparkling drops on the rocks below. Lewis, certain now that he was on the Missouri, summoned the rest of the party forward. He called the falls "the grandest sight I ever beheld."

But the falls proved as troublesome as they were beautiful. The boats, of course, could not travel through them, and so had to be carried around them, a job that required two weeks. The weather did nothing to help matters. It alternated between blazing heat and sudden storms. Once, a storm dumped hail the size of small rocks on the men, cutting some and knocking others down. Late in June, a cloudburst drove Clark, Sacajawea, and Charbonneau to take shelter beneath an overhanging rock in a narrow ravine. Moments later, Clark shouted with alarm when he saw a wall of water rushing down the surrounding hills and into the ravine. The trio climbed to safety just seconds before their shelter disappeared beneath fifteen feet of muddy, swirling water.

Beyond the falls, the Missouri ran wide and smooth for a time, allowing several days of tranquil sailing. Then, narrowing again, the river ripped its way between sheer granite cliffs. Lewis and Clark agreed that they had never seen such lonely country. They traveled for weeks without once glimpsing anyone other than their own men. But there was game everywhere, particularly big-horned sheep that darted along the cliff tops and stared down at the intruders' canoes.

Most astonishing, though, were the beavers of the area. Some of their patiently built dams, often five or more feet high, imprisoned as much as five acres of water.

Deep in Montana, the river jogged north and then turned sharply west and south, bringing the explorers to the area now known as Three Forks. At this point little more than a fast-flowing creek, the Missouri joined what were to be called the Beaverhead, Madison, and Gallatin rivers. And here the Missouri came to an end, with Lewis and Clark finding its source along a tiny nearby stream, which they christened in honor of Thomas Jefferson. They looked at each other and knew that one day they would have to tell the president that the Missouri could never serve as a water highway connecting the Pacific coast with the midlands of America. Then they looked west to the towering Bitterroot Range of the Rocky Mountains. How far beyond those great walls lay the Pacific? They wondered.

The Shoshone Indians living in the Three Forks area also looked west to the mountains and then at the explorers' canoes. Those little boats would never do for the next leg of the journey. Pack animals were needed. Quickly, the Shoshones collected and presented to Lewis and Clark a string of horses.

It seemed to the two travelers that the Shoshones were the friendliest of the Indians they had yet encountered. And friendly they should be, for Sacajawea was one of their own, and the expedition had brought her home to them. There were smiles upon her arrival and then tears of joy, followed by much feasting and dancing when she was reunited with her brother, young Chief Cumeahwait.

As soon as the homecoming celebration ended, the explorers transferred their gear from the canoes to the pack horses. They were impatient to be on their way, for autumn was at hand, and they wanted to be clear of the Bitterroots before winter closed in. To be trapped in ice and snow high in those mountains, they knew, meant but one thing— death. As Lewis and Clark made ready to leave, they were surprised and gratified to hear Sacajawea say that she intended to accompany them. She felt that there was much valuable work that she could still do for the expedition. And, besides, she was as eager as they to see the Pacific. She would come back to her people when the trip was completed.

The journey over the Bitterroot Range presented the explorers with one danger after another. High winds lashed them, often knocking them back against granite walls, and brief snowstorms blinded them and chilled them to the bone. More than once the edge of the trail underfoot gave way and sent one or more of the pack animals hurtling down to their deaths. Little or no game wandered into view. Food ran low, while the men longingly recalled the earlier days of plenty. Soon, they had to kill several of the horses for food. Whenever they looked up, they saw mountains that seemed to be higher than those they had already crossed. The men began to wonder if they were destined to roam through these high altitudes with their lungs aching in the cold, thin air, for the rest of their days. Then, one afternoon, they heard a shout from Clark, who was hiking up ahead. They hurried forward to where he stood on a peak that seemed thrust right against the sky. He was smiling, and they immediately saw why. Spread out below was a mountain plain—the vast Clearwater Valley in what is now the state of Idaho.

The party had defeated the Bitterroots. Once they had made their way down to the sheltered valley, they met its friendly and welcoming residents, the Nez Perce Indians. After the agonizingly slow passage through the Bitterroots, the journey through the valley seemed to proceed at a breakneck speed. The Nez Perces, hearing that the explorers were heading west, outfitted them with canoes and pointed them along the valley's Clearwater River, saying that it soon joined the mighty and westward-running Snake River. True to the Indians' words, the explorers soon reached the Snake and shot quickly along it until it joined an even mightier river in what was one day to be the state of Washington.

This was the great Columbia River. It bore the party steadily west along what is now the Oregon-Washington border, carrying them first through a stretch of wild, foaming rapids and then along a wide and almost silky waterway. The explorers' spirits ran high, for every day seemed an enchanted one. The autumn sunlight splintered itself on the great trees lining the banks of the river and stretching back out of sight. Startled birds screeched at the approach of the canoes and the birds' wings beat the clear air with the sound of a thousand muted drums. Game peered out from the trees, and fish glittered, silvery and fleeting, just below the river's surface. And, best of all, there was the signal that the sea was near—gulls, wheeling overhead in great, lazy circles.

And at last there was the scent of the ocean in the air, growing stronger by the hour and driving the men to dig the paddles deeper and faster into the cool river water.

On November 15, 1805, the canoes swept out of the Columbia and into a great bay. Now the scent of the sea was overpowering, and far across the bay, at the point where it opened out into a seemingly endless expanse of blue-green water, there were breakers, rolling gently and foaming white. The men rested at their oars. Lewis and Clark sat hushed. A journey of eighteen months and close to four thousand miles was finished. They had come to the Pacific Ocean.

Lewis and Clark turned to look at their men and to signal them forward. Again, strong arms dug paddles into the water. The breakers drew steadily closer.

Lewis and Clark remained alongside the Pacific until March 26, 1806. Then they retraced their steps home, taking time to explore the Yellowstone and Marias rivers and to bid farewell to Sacajawea when she rejoined her people. Lewis and Clark reached St. Louis on September 23.

Jefferson, as did everyone in the young United States, welcomed the explorers as heroes. News of the many wonders that they had brought home with them from the West spread far and wide, as did their descriptions of the Indians they had met and the magnificent lands they had seen. Honors came to them from all directions, climaxed by their appointments to highly responsible government positions. Lewis was named governor of the northern area of the Louisiana Territory, a post he held until his death, in 1809, at the early age of thirty-four. To Clark went the job of Missouri's territorial governor. He served in that capacity from 1813 to 1821 and then as Superintendent of Indian Affairs at St. Louis until 1838, the year of his death.

Wherever word of Lewis and Clark traveled, enthusiasm for the American West blossomed. Explorers and woods-men—among them Jim Bridger, Zebulon Pike, and John C. Fremont—pressed into the wilds to see for themselves the beauty and bounty there. They were soon followed, as are all trailblazers, by the settlers—the farmers, the cattlemen, the merchants and businessmen, the artists and artisans, the teachers, the laborers, the housewives, and the children—all the people who turn a wilderness into a civilization.

Because of the work of two men and their forty-five followers a nation was forged to its western shores.

Part Three

5

Australasia

It is a vast region. It stretches across the Pacific Ocean
south from the equator to latitude 47°. Within its confines
are 3.3 million square miles of land surrounded by great
expanses of a sea that is sometimes calm and sparkling in the
sun, and sometimes wild and wind-tossed beneath fast-run-
ning, leaden clouds. In its day, it has been the setting for
exploration, trade, piracy, colonization, and, during World
War II, intense and cruel fighting.

Geographers long ago gave it one of the most romantic
of names—Australasia.

The region is not all of one piece, but is divided into
thousands of islands sprinkled throughout the South Pacific.
Some are mere humps of coral and sand thrusting up from
the sea. Some are members of the sprawling Malay Archi-
pelago. Some bear names known everywhere—Tasmania,
New Zealand, Tahiti, Easter Island, Christmas Island, the
New Hebrides, the Marquesas, the Fiji Islands, and the
Samoan Islands. One is simultaneously the world's largest
island and smallest continent—Australia.

The South Pacific's principal native inhabitants are the
Melanesians, the Polynesians, and Australia's Aborigines.
The Melanesians are a smallish, dark-skinned, dark-haired
people whose general physical characteristics have caused
many anthropologists to classify them as members of the
Negro race. The Polynesians are large-framed, brown-faced,
and brown-eyed. Their hair is deep black, often straight,
and just as often wavy. Oddly, at times it may show streaks
of blond. The Aborigines are generally recognized by their
long, small skulls, their broad faces and noses, and their
small chins. Their coloring ranges from reddish brown to
dark brown.

Anthropologists believe that the Melanesians and Polynesians originally came from somewhere in southeast Asia,
sailing their rafts and canoes deep into the Pacific and settling down on the islands that fell across their bows. The
Melanesians selected such islands as the New Hebrides and
the Fiji and Solomon groups, while the Polynesians chose
such places as Tahiti, Easter Island, the Marquesas, and the
Samoas. Some Polynesians even ventured as far north as the
Hawaiian Islands, and it is theorized that others sailed all
the way east to South America. One Polynesian band, the
Maoris, landed at New Zealand and came ashore, so their
legends say, in 1350 A.D. at the close of a journey south from
Tahiti. Once landed, they found and overcame a race of
New Zealand inhabitants whose origins are unknown to us.

Also a mystery to us is the origin of the Aborigines. Their
homeland is Australia. Anthropologists have been unable to
determine a connection between them and any other race
and so have designated them as a separate race called Austra-
loid. Some anthropologists contend that, as did the Melanesians and Polynesians, the Aborigines originally lived

in Asia. This belief is based upon similarities noted between the ways of the Aborigines and those of certain hill tribes in India. Other anthropologists conjecture that the Aborigines may be descendants of Neanderthal man. Whatever their origin, the Aborigines remain much a part of Australia today, a tallish, proud race of hunters and food gatherers.

Several million native people call Australasia home—and have called it home for centuries. But until Magellan and those who followed him pushed their way into the Pacific the presence of all these people and their almost countless islands was unknown to the Europeans. In fact, the Europeans harbored a totally mistaken notion even of what Australasia looked like.

The mistake began with the ancient Greeks. They theorized that there must be a giant continent down at the bottom of the world. There *had* to be such a continent, they reasoned. The world needed it as a balance against all the sprawling land masses and heavy winds to the north.

This untested idea survived through the centuries and then was given credence when Magellan, while fighting his way around the foot of South America, looked south and saw the land that his sailors named Tierra del Fuego because of its mysterious fires. Later explorations proved Tierra del Fuego to be an island, but, in the meantime, cartographers assumed that it must be the northern shoreline of the land that the Greeks had envisioned. Into their maps went the imagined outlines of a vast southern continent.

Their continent blanketed all of the bottom of the world. They named it Terra Australis and, on the basis of rumor and sheer fancy, endowed its coastline with two giant, northward-thrusting humps. One pushed its way deep into the

Indian Ocean and was called Brasilie Regio. The other,
christened Patalis Regio, was coincidentally drawn in the
area now occupied by Australia.

Once Magellan had broken into the Pacific, other explorers quickly made their way there, all of them with any
combination of three aims in mind—to chart new sea lanes
to the Orient, to harvest the riches waiting on lands en
route, and to determine the presence and actual shape of
Terra Australis. Thanks to their discoveries and charting,
the explorers persistently cut away at the boundaries of the
mythical land mass and replaced them with Australasia's
many islands and its continents of Australia and Antarctica.

The cutting up of Terra Australis into islands began in
1567, when two Spanish ships, commanded by Alvaro de
Mendana and outward bound from Peru, came upon the
Solomon Islands. Mendana spent six months there in search
of gold, earning only the attacks of cannibal natives that
finally made him run for home. He returned in 1595, this
time discovering and putting on the map the Marquesas
Islands and Santa Cruz, one of the northernmost islands in
the New Hebrides group. A decade later, Pedro Fernandez
de Quiros, who had been Mendana's second-in-command,
further charted the New Hebrides and anchored for several
weeks at the group's main island, which he christened
Espiritu Santo.

One of Quiros's captains, Luis Vaez de Torres, is believed
to have made the white man's first sighting of Australia at
this time. From the New Hebrides he sailed west until he
reached the Great Barrier Reef, which lies off Australia's
present-day Queensland. De Torres ventured past the reef
and through what has since been named Torres Strait. To
his north lay the southern shores of New Guinea (both the
Spanish and the Portuguese had visited its northern side

earlier, with the latter naming it New Guinea because its frizzy-haired inhabitants reminded them of the natives found on Africa's Guinea coast), and to his south loomed what is now Cape York, Australia's northernmost point of land. De Torres failed to realize that he was literally within arm's reach of a sprawling continent and sailed on without pausing to investigate it.

At the dawn of the seventeenth century, the Dutch, who were then conducting a lively trade with ports along the Indian Ocean, began to push east into the Pacific. Their search was for new markets, but they did much to shrink the size of Terra Australis. Their first voyages sighted no land where the maps of the day said Brasilie Regio should be, and so the maps had to undergo a major revision, with Brasilie Regio starting on the path to its eventual disappearance. As for the Patalis Regio bulge, Dutch skippers did find land there, glimpsing but not landing at the barren west coast of Australia. Then, in 1642, Dutch Captain Abel Tasman demonstrated that Patalis Regio must be some sort of gargantuan island when he sailed around it to the south and discovered the islands of Tasmania and, over to the east, New Zealand. Tasman cruised along just a portion of New Zealand's western shoreline, thus failing to learn that it is really two islands. Instead, Tasman surmised that New Zealand must mark the beginnings of Terra Australis.

Late in the seventeenth century, England became interested in the South Pacific, thanks to the pirate captain William Dampier, who spent more than a month in 1688 off the northwestern Australian coast and then, a few years later, charted the northern shores of New Guinea and discovered the island of New Britain. Elsewhere, the Dutch were still patiently hacking away at the borders of Terra Australis, with one of the biggest cuts being made by Captain Jacob Roggeveen. In 1722, at the place where continental land was supposed to be, Roggeveen discovered Easter Island and the Samoas.

By the middle of the eighteenth century, the nations interested in the South Pacific knew full well that the Terra Australis of old was fast dwindling away to nothing, and that, to date, it had been reshaped into a series of islands, one of their number so large that it might be a continent itself. But, though the years had seen some fine exploratory work, much information on the vast region was still needed. The nations wanted more precise charts of the various islands already found. They wanted data on the native peoples there, on the plant and animal and marine life, on the natural resources, and on the possibilities for future trade and colonization.

And, of course, they wanted to know more about the southern areas yet unexplored. Did New Zealand, they asked, really mark the beginnings of Terra Australis? Or was it an island with a great sea beyond it? And, if so, was there any land—any continent or any islands—at the bottom of the world, down in the region of the South Pole?

The information that was needed seemed limitless. It was information that could best be collected by a man who was not only an explorer but a scientist as well, a man different from all the Spanish conquerors, Dutch traders, and English adventurers who had gone before him. History had set the stage for the entrance of the quiet Captain James Cook.

6

Captain James Cook

ENGLAND HAD A MIGHTY ADVENTURE in mind during the summer of 1768. A transit of Venus across the face of the sun was due on July 1 of the following year, and seven British scientists were readying themselves for a journey into the far South Pacific to observe it. Their destination was Tahiti, where calculations indicated that the passage of the planet would best be seen. The scientists were to travel in the ship *Endeavor*.

The British Admiralty had purchased and refitted the vessel especially for the voyage at a cost of £5,000. It was to be manned by eighty-four sailors. In command would be forty-year-old James Cook, a Royal Navy veteran just promoted to the rank of lieutenant.

Not one scientist in England disputed the choice of Cook to lead the enterprise. He was known as a superb seaman and navigator, a fine organizer, and a man of boundless energy. But best of all, he was recognized as a man of scientific bent.

That Cook had been named commander of the *Endeavor*

and that, indeed, he had attained the rank of lieutenant in the navy was a clear testament to his ability. For his was a day and age when promotion in the military depended primarily upon wealth and an important family name. Cook began life with neither asset. His only weapons were his intelligence, his energy, and—surprising in a man whose nature was gentle and quiet—his driving ambition. Of the latter, Cook would one day write that he had always wanted "not only to go farther than any man had ever been before, but as far as possible for a man to go."

Cook's beginnings were humble. Born on October 28, 1728, at the Yorkshire village of Marton, he was the son of a farm worker, who apprenticed him to a haberdasher at age twelve and then to a coastal shipping company when the boy was in his teens. For the company, young Cook sailed in coal traders to Norway and the Baltic, rising from seaman to ship's mate.

But Cook wanted more than a life in blackened coal ships, and he joined the Royal Navy at age twenty-seven. Within four years, he had won his master's papers and had ventured into the New World, establishing his reputation not only as a fine officer but also as an able surveyor, cartographer, and astronomer. With Royal Navy expeditions, Cook charted the lower St. Lawrence River and the coasts of Newfoundland and Labrador. Then, in 1766, on a small island just off Newfoundland's Cape Ray, he observed a solar eclipse and published an account of what he had seen.

Yes, the scientists agreed, the right leader had been chosen for the Tahiti venture—an all-round seaman and scientist. For the voyage was not intended merely to observe the transit of Venus. It was also to sail down to New Zealand, chart its coastline, and determine whether New Zealand was part of the Terra Australis continent. En route—in fact,

Captain James Cook

wherever it went—the expedition was to collect all possible data on every aspect of the South Pacific's life and geography.

The *Endeavor* raised sail on August 25, 1768, rounded the foot of South America, and proceeded northwest to Tahiti, anchoring off its palm-fringed beaches on April 13, 1769. The journey passed quietly under Cook's gentle command, with the crewmen fishing over the side and the scientists examining with interest the sea life and seaweed that was dropped to the deck. At Tahiti, the scientists observed the transit of Venus, and the botanists among them— particularly twenty-five-year-old Joseph Banks, who was destined to become one of England's most respected scientists and statesmen—stored one plant specimen after another aboard. Cook spent much of his time studying the natives and the geography of the island.

From Tahiti, he turned the *Endeavor* southwest for New Zealand, immediately discovering and pausing to explore and chart the Society Islands. Weeks later, Cook arrived at the east coast of what is now known as New Zealand's North Island. For the next six months, he slowly circumnavigated both the North Island and its sister South Island, passing through the strait that separates them and that now bears his name. All the while, Cook carefully charted his course and gave the world its first accurate outline of New Zealand. His work destroyed the old suspicion that New Zealand was a part of Terra Australis. From all sides of the two islands, the sea stretched away to the horizon.

Cook intended that the next step in his voyage should take him westward to Tasmania, at that time known as Van Diemen's Land. En route, however, a storm closed over the *Endeavor* and drove the ship off course, pushing it so far to the north that, when the skies cleared, Cook found himself off the southeastern tip of Australia. He probed north along the continent's coast, noted its similarity to the Welsh area of Glamorganshire, and christened it New South Wales. At last, Cook came upon a large and shallow bay. He entered it to take on water and smiled as he heard the botanists aboard insist that it should be named Botany Bay.

Cook remembered the moments of entering Botany Bay as being among the strangest of the entire voyage. As the *Endeavor* slid across the quiet waters, it passed two natives fishing in a canoe. They looked up at its immense spread of white sails but, instead of fleeing in terror, hardly lifted an eyebrow before turning back to their fishing. A short time later, when Cook and thirty men came ashore from two small boats, they encountered two more natives—this time a pair who greeted them with poised spears and angry cries. Cook sent them running when he ordered muskets fired over their heads.

During the next days, ever on the lookout for unfriendly natives, Cook made several exploratory trips ashore, on one of them hiking up to the place where the southern outskirts of the city of Sydney are now to be found. Then he continued his voyage northward along the eastern face of the continent, carefully mapping the shoreline as he went, but somehow managing to miss the great harbor that serves modern Sydney. In a matter of a few weeks, Cook lay up against the vast stretch of coral that is the Great Barrier Reef.

He inched his way through the reef, damaged the *Endeavor*'s hull on an outcropping of coral, and pulled up to the shore to make repairs. Here Cook and Joseph Banks were astonished to see a strange animal come loping through the brush—an animal that moved on great hind legs while holding its small forepaws close to its chest. Western man was taking his first look at the kangaroo.

With the *Endeavor* again seaworthy, Cook edged his way east through the strait that de Torres had come upon more than a century earlier. Unlike de Torres, however, Cook paid close attention to the shores to either side, charting both the southern New Guinea and the northern Australian coasts. Once clear of the strait, Cook continued westward to Batavia and then across the Indian Ocean and around the Cape of Good Hope to close his voyage by sailing north through the Atlantic to England. He arrived home on June 12, 1771.

One of the most fruitful voyages in history was ended. In the holds of the *Endeavor* were countless specimens of South Pacific plant and geologic life. In the vessel's chartrooms were accurate charts of thousands of miles of hitherto mysterious seas and their islands. And in the diaries of the *Endeavor's* captain and scientists were words that eloquently described the people of Australasia, their customs, their outlooks, and the riches of their lands. Available to all the world was the knowledge that the mythical Terra Australis had grown even smaller, that New Zealand was not a part of its shoreline, and that Australia was revealing itself as a giant island continent that might one day beckon colonists.

James Cook had led an expedition that had erased much of the remaining mystery from Australasia and had replaced ignorance with fact. Explorers traveling in Cook's wake would now be armed with accurate maps and accurate descriptions of the islands and peoples they would en-counter. Cook and his company had done what all explorers hope to do—they had turned strange lands and waters into familiar lands and waters.

But Cook's work was not yet done. He was promoted to the rank of commander and then to that of captain and as-signed to two more voyages. The first, which was made between 1772 and 1774, took him deep into southern waters in search of the last remnants of Terra Australis; we shall hear more of it in a later chapter on the Antarctic. The second voyage began in 1776 and, after carrying Cook down around the Cape of Good Hope, sent him eastward across the Indian Ocean and then northward through the Pacific to the Hawaiian Islands, then called the Sandwich Islands. From there, he ventured northeast and explored the upper reaches of the North American coastline to the Bering Strait. He passed through the strait, but soon had to turn back because of ice. He returned to the Hawaiian group via the Asian coast.

There, on what is now the main island of Hawaii, an unforeseen and minor incident ended Captain Cook's life. On the night of February 13, 1779, while Cook was anchored at Kealakekua Bay, several natives made off with one of his ship's boats. Cook led a contingent of seamen ashore in the morning, his plan being to take a native king prisoner and hold him until the boat was returned. The king's subjects, however, closed angrily about the white men and Cook ordered a retreat. At the water's edge, a native struck him from behind with a club. Cook fell but rose quickly to defend himself. Instantly, he was surrounded by flashing clubs and spears, and before a single one of his men could come to his aid, he lay dead in the sand.

Closed, abruptly and tragically, was one of the greatest careers in exploration. Historians have long pondered on the work that Cook might have accomplished had he lived. He was fifty-one at the time of his death, and assuredly many active years of exploration still lay ahead of him. What lands might he have found? What seas might he have charted? What scientific notes might he have made? We cannot even guess.

All that we can say is that, in the time that was granted to him, Cook accomplished what we might well expect of a whole company of gifted men. He taught the world much of the geography of the South Pacific. He told people everywhere of its multifarious human, animal, plant, geologic, and marine life. He played a major role in replacing the fantasy of Terra Australis with the fact of Australasia.

In so doing, James Cook opened the way to the colonization of Australia and New Zealand and to the birth of the modern South Pacific.

Part Four

7

Africa

THE GIANT LAND MASS called Africa lies directly south across the Mediterranean Sea from Europe. Its western shores face the Atlantic, while its east coast looks on the Indian Ocean and stretches to touch western Asia. In size, it is the world's fourth largest continent, with approximately 11.5 million square miles of jungles, mountains, plateaus, vast grasslands, and sandy deserts contained within its borders. For hundreds of years, right up to our own century, outsiders have looked upon Africa as a wild and mysterious land. So little has been known about it that long ago it earned the name "The Dark Continent."

It seems odd at first glance that Africa was so long considered a mysterious continent, for its northern region was the seat of one of the world's earliest, greatest, and best-known nations. Along the Nile River, the civilization that was Egypt took shape some five thousand years before the birth of Christ—a civilization about which countless books have been written, a civilization that could read and write and construct breathtaking buildings and monuments while the people of central Europe were still primitive nomads, and a civilization that traded with all the other Mediterranean countries of the day.

And the fact that the continent was so long shrouded in mystery seems doubly odd when we read of the ambitious explorations that marked the early history of Africa.

In 600 B.C., Egypt's King Necho asked the best of all ancient sailors, the Phoenicians, to voyage completely round the continent and bring back word of its general shape. The Phoenicians sailed down the eastern coast from the Gulf of Aqaba, rounded the bottom of the continent, and advanced north through the Atlantic to return to Egypt via the Straits of Gibraltar, at that time called the Pillars of Hercules. Thus, ancient seamen navigated the Cape of Good Hope almost twenty-one centuries before Portugal's Bartholomew Diaz came along.

And remember that Necho had asked the Phoenicians to sail "round" the continent. His request suggests that, somehow, the general shape of Africa was already known, if only vaguely, in his time. How could a land have been mysterious when its general outline was known at least—and perhaps more than—six hundred years before the birth of Christ?

Almost a century and a half after Necho's time, Hanno of Carthage led a voyage of Phoenicians out through the Pillars of Hercules and south to the Gulf of Guinea, which now fronts Nigeria, the Cameroons, and the Gold and Ivory coasts. Hanno landed and pushed inland until the sight of distant bonfires and the sound of native drums sent him hurrying back to his ships and the open sea. Later, Greek explorers retraced Hanno's steps to the gulf. Going ashore at the Ivory Coast, the Greeks befriended the natives and launched a trade that was to endure for many years—a trade that saw magnificently loomed African cloths and fine wood carvings find their way to Greece.

Nor were all the explorations of Africa limited to its coast. Some probed deep inland. The Greek explorer and geographer Strabo, who lived between 66 B.C. and 24 A.D., visited the African interior during his lifetime. He ventured south from Egypt and entered the land of Ethiopia, finding the way of life of its inhabitants "wretched." Of them, Strabo wrote that "they are for the most part naked and wander from place to place with their flocks" of sheep, goats, and oxen. Others, he reported, "hunt elephants, lions, and panthers." He visited Ethiopia's principal city, Meroe, and also saw copper, gold, and iron mines. He said that "palm, the persea [peach], ebony, and carob trees are found in abundance."

Four hundred years later, European missionaries came to Ethiopia. They not only established Christianity there but also spent the next centuries exploring through and beyond the country. One of the missionaries, Father Paez, even made his way to the source of the Blue Nile River. He disproved the old idea that the annual flooding of this river, which pours into and helps flood the mighty Nile of Egypt, is caused by melting mountain snow, showing instead that the heavy downpours of the rainy season are responsible.

Far away, in what was to become French West Africa, later explorers pushed inland and collected a great deal of information. In 1352, the great Arab explorer Ibn-Batuta, who is said to have traveled at least seventy-five thousand miles in his seventy-three-year lifetime, set out south from Tangiers on the northwestern coast and made his way down to the West African cities of Timbuktu and Gao on the Niger River. Here, he found himself in the heart of the

great black African empire of Songhai, or Sornhai. It had
been growing since before the time of Christ and had
reached a far more advanced level of civilization than had
many a European nation. The cities of Songhai were
adorned with fine buildings and paved and tree-lined streets.
Great monuments were seen everywhere, as were schools
and universities. The people, whom Ibn-Batuta described
as "admirable" and "just," governed themselves by a strict
set of laws.

Timbuktu welcomed another visitor almost two centuries
later. He was Johannes Leo, a Moorish nobleman popularly
called Leo Africanus because of his writings about the continent. On his visit, Africanus was impressed with Songhai's
grain, milk, and butter production and with the education
and ability of the empire's doctors, scholars, priests, and
judges. He commented that books ranked high among the
country's imports.

All these explorers, missionaries, and traders mapped the
places they visited and wrote accounts of their experiences.
A wealth of material on Africa was collected through the
passing centuries. How then, after this fine start at exploration, did the continent lose itself in a cloud of mystery? What
happened to all the writings about Africa? Why did men
not move right on from its known to its unknown regions?
How did it come to be the "Dark Continent?"

The answer is to be found in the wars that rent the centuries following the birth of Christ. First, as we saw earlier,
barbarian hordes overran Europe. Slaughtering anyone
who got in their way, they terrified the people, driving them
to huddle inside the walls of their cities. Exploration and
trade withered in the flames of violence. Few Europeans
wanted to abandon the safety of their hearths, even for rich
Africa.

Then, in the eleventh century, Europe mobilized the Crusades to free the Holy Land of Palestine from the grasp of the conquering Turks. European Christian thought considered the Turks, who were of the Islamic faith, to be heathens. Africa was considered a part of the Turkish realm and so it, too, was regarded as heathen. Europeans wanted no part of it. Africa was a vile place, to be avoided at all costs.

The result: Europeans forgot or ignored all that had been so painstakingly learned about the continent. They showed no interest in learning about its vast, as-yet-unexplored regions. To the Europeans, Africa became a strange and wild land, savage and dangerous. The "Dark Continent" was born.

Europeans shunned Africa until the fifteenth century. By that time, the violence in Europe had subsided. The spirit of exploration was blossoming again, and European adventurers were looking east to the fabulous markets of the Orient. It was then that Portugal's Prince Henry the Navigator ordered his captains south to try to find their way eastward around the tip of Africa. En route, they discovered a thriving commerce along the Atlantic face of the continent, a commerce in gold and ivory and slaves that Arab traders had been conducting for hundreds of years. Immediately, Portugal took a share of this trade and was soon joined by other nations. The next decades saw the north and west shores of Africa become familiar and profitable grounds for European traders.

Particularly profitable was the traffic in slaves. For centuries, Africa had been the chief source of slaves for nearby Asian nations. Now it served the same function for Europe and the New World. Thousands of terrified natives were snatched from their inland villages and driven by Arab—and

even African—slavers to coastal ports, where they were
crammed in the filthy holds of ships for trips to all points of
the globe.

The eighteenth century saw a reawakening of interest in
the interior of the African continent. Explorers wondered
what natural resources and what kinds of people they could
find in all those northern and western areas visited long
ago by Ibn-Batuta, Leo Africanus, and the Jesuit Paez. They
were particularly curious about those thousands of miles of
unexplored country to the south, and they chose to carry
out their explorations along Africa's greatest rivers.

Far to the north, James Bruce of Scotland mapped his
way for hundreds of miles along the Nile River. Then England's John Speke traveled all the way to Lake Victoria and
its little Kagera River, the sources of the mighty Nile.

Over toward the west, Mungo Park made two trips—in
1795 and 1805—along the Niger River of the old Songhai
civilization. Park was able to follow the river for only a few
miles during his first journey, an adventure in which he was
plagued by an Arab tribe and a band of robbers. The Arabs
held him captive for four months, and then, as Park was
working his way back to safety, the robbers attacked him
and stripped him of all his possessions except his shirt.

On his second journey, Park followed the Niger for several hundred miles until tragedy overtook him at Bussa
Rapids. Here, when his boat became lodged in the rocks, a
tribe of savage natives lined the banks and unleashed a rain
of arrows on him. In a desperate attempt to escape, Park
and his companions dove into the rapids. All but one, a
native servant, drowned.

Later in the nineteenth century, other explorers completed the work that Park had begun. Men such as France's
Rene Caillie, England's Richard Lander, and Germany's

Heinrich Barth traced the Niger all along its meandering path through West Africa to its mouth at the Gulf of Guinea.

To the south, missionaries in the nineteenth century pushed two hundred miles up the great Congo River. Barth came down from West Africa to cross the Congo's watershed and travel along one of the river's tributaries.

Because of these and other explorers, Africa's northern and western regions and great chunks of its central area down to and beyond the Congo became fairly well known by the middle of the nineteenth century. The body of knowledge that these men had thus far assembled began to attract settlers and missionaries in greater and greater numbers. Most of the settlers built towns and trading posts along the coasts, while some of their number ventured inland to try their hand at trading with the natives, hunting, farming, and mining. The missionaries pushed inland to doctor the natives and to teach them the ways of the Christian faith.

Exploration of the vast southern area of the continent—an area including the long Zambezi River—had barely begun at this time. Among the missionaries was a man who would contribute much to that exploration. His name was David Livingstone.

8

David Livingstone

THE MAN WHO WAS to become one of the greatest explorers in the history of Africa did not, at first, want to go there. Rather, he hoped to work in China.

But the officials at the London Missionary Society had other plans for Dr. David Livingstone of Scotland. They began by telling him that there were no available posts in the Orient. Then they turned to a wall map of southern Africa, their eyes settling on the little flag that marked the mission site at Kuruman in Bechuanaland. Somewhere near there, they said, was where he was needed.

And so it was a disappointed medical missionary who came down the gangway when the ship from England docked at Algoa Bay in early 1841. David Livingstone was twenty-seven years old at the time, a tall and slender man with dark hair and finely chiseled features. According to his friends, his tastes were simple, his manner was gentle, and his desire to help the helpless, fierce. They added with a smile that he was possibly the most impatient fellow they had ever met. He could not tolerate delay of any sort. A job that needed to be done had to be done immediately.

Characteristically, Livingstone did not linger at Algoa Bay, which pokes into the shore at the eastern end of the Cape of Good Hope, but started inland immediately. His Bechuanaland destination lay more than two hundred miles north, up on the plateau that blankets most of the African continent, and, with his every step, he felt his old ambition to work in China slipping from him. All that he saw in this wild land fascinated him.

And there was so much to see—grassy velds stretching away endlessly; strange trees and plants, some bursting with leaves, others twisted and naked in the wind; swift rivers and lazy streams. Everywhere Livingstone looked, there was wildlife—scorpions darting underfoot; porcupines waddling across his trail; squirrels flitting up tree trunks and staring at him without a blink as he passed by; hyenas foraging in the underbrush; antelopes vaulting against the horizon; elephants lumbering; zebras grazing.

All was fascinating—and much was appalling. There were the native villages—huts of mud and thatch, with bugs and rodents scuttling among them. The huts had earthen floors and open fires that sent forth thick, yellowish smoke and the odors of eternal cooking. The people, all wide-eyed with curiosity, gathered to see the passing white man. Many of them were bent and twisted, bloated, or scarred and pocked with the diseases and injuries of primitive life.

Here, Livingstone thought, was a land to challenge any man. He knew that he was up to the challenge. The hardships of his own life had made him equal to it.

Livingstone had been born to poverty on March 19, 1813, in the village of Blantyre. His family was so poor that he had gone to work in a cotton mill at age ten to help support it. The hours and the work, stretching from dawn to dark, had been enough to break even a full-grown man. But the

difficulties he encountered did not break him. He was ambitious. Nothing would stop him from doing something
with his life.

When Livingstone was in his teens, he decided that he
wanted to be a doctor and a minister so that he could travel
out as a missionary to help the world's more unfortunate
people.

Doctor! Minister! They seemed impossible goals for an
unlettered young mill hand. Both professions required long
university training. And no one could hope to enter a university without money or a proper basic education. Livingstone had neither.

But he would not be stopped. He attended night school
and saved all that he could from his meager earnings. At
twenty-two years of age, he was able to enroll at Anderson
College in Glasgow and attend his first classes in medicine
and theology. From there, he went on to become a member
of the London Missionary Society in 1838 and to take his
medical degree at Glasgow's Faculty of Physicians and Sur-
geons in 1840, only a year before his arrival in Africa.

Indeed, he was equal to any challenge that Africa could
offer. Arriving at Kuruman, he paused briefly and then
pushed farther north, looking for just the right place to
establish his first mission station. Livingstone ended his
search in the valley of Mabotsa. He unpacked his medical
gear, built a cabin for himself, and began his work with
the natives, explaining the Gospel to them and tending their
ills and injuries, all the while learning their language and
making endless notes on their customs.

In their turn, the natives took Livingstone to their hearts,
as was to happen wherever he went in Africa. The natives
realized he was a genuine friend, one who wanted only to
help them and one who did not peer down his nose at their

David Livingstone

primitive ways. Soon his reputation was such that many a Mabotsa family would trudge one hundred and thirty miles or more to place themselves in his healing care.

Livingstone remained in the valley for two years. During that time he married Mary Moffat, whose father had built the mission at Kuruman, and she happily joined her husband in his work, her tasks proving to be many and varied. She served as nurse when he performed surgery. She helped him instruct the natives in religion. And, on her own, Mary organized classes in art, sewing, and cooking for the women. She fully expected to give the rest of her life to the valley.

But not so Livingstone—he was dreaming a new dream for himself. In addition to his regular duties, he spent much time exploring the country round about, sometimes venturing more than a hundred miles from home. He found that exploration excited him and that he much preferred it to the day-by-day routine at the mission. Livingstone began to see himself as a missionary who would hike into unknown areas, befriend the natives, and establish missions that would then be operated by others.

Such a man, he told himself, could be of vital service to Africa. Vast regions of the continent had yet to see their first missionary and had yet even to be placed on a map. Livingstone could be the first missionary to those regions, blazing a trail for others to follow. And he could be the first mapmaker, illuminating this thrilling land for all to see. He resolved to devote himself to exploration at the earliest possible moment.

His chance to explore did not come until 1849, after he had built two mission stations beyond the valley. In that year, Livingstone traveled far north through Bechuanaland to Lake Ngami, which no white man had ever visited. En route, he crossed the sandy inferno called the Kalahari Desert. Daily heat mirages there intrigued him, and the living conditions of the desert's Bushmen residents sickened him.

A diminutive, nomadic people, the Bushmen spent their lives hunting and scratching the baked earth for food and were bone-thin from lack of nourishment. They wore loincloths, used tools that dated back to the Stone Age, and knew practically nothing of medical care. They fled at the sight of any stranger, for they were terrified of the slave traders who regularly invaded their land and, whips in hand, snatched away their loved ones.

When Livingstone returned home, he gave the world its

first detailed, written account of the Kalahari and, thanks to his careful charting, filled in much of the map of this barren African region. His career as an explorer was officially launched.

In 1851, accompanied by Mary and their children, he undertook an even longer journey, hiking for more than a thousand miles over mountains and through jungles to the Zambezi River on the border of Bechuanaland and Rhodesia. He planned to establish a mission for the river's Makololo tribe, but, as soon as he arrived, he knew that he could not remain for long. Here, deep in the interior of the continent, at a point almost exactly midway between the Atlantic on one side and the Indian Ocean on the other, Livingstone found himself in swamp country. The air was hot and thick and damp, filled with mosquitoes and tsetse flies, the latter carrying the deadly sleeping sickness in their bite. Fearing for his family's health, Livingstone retreated home.

But he knew that he must return to the Zambezi as soon as possible. For, while there, he had been struck with an idea —an inspiration, really, possibly the most important thought of his career. This was even more significant than his idea to become an exploring missionary.

The inspiration had to do with using the Zambezi to help end the centuries-old African traffic in slaves, a traffic that Livingstone had loathed since the very day he had come down from the ship in Algoa Bay ten long years earlier.

Everywhere in those years, Livingstone had seen the horrors of slavery. He had seen bent, half-naked men working the plantations and mines of the Boer settlers on the Cape of Good Hope. He had seen the burned ruins of native villages after slave raids. He had seen long slave caravans, their chained victims—men, women, and children alike—weeping as they were driven to the coastal ports to be crammed into the airless holds of ships for the journey to the markets of North and South America. Livingstone knew that, for every hundred slaves who reached their final destination, at least a thousand others died along the way.

He hated the practice, and he had spoken out against it time and again. His words had done nothing but earn him the hate of many Boer settlers.

Practical Scot that he was, Livingstone knew that all the talk in the world would never eliminate the horrible traffic. It was much too profitable a business to wither before mere words. The only solution was to replace the slave traffic with a legitimate trade. The interior of Africa teemed with natural resources and with native goods and works of art. If a trade in these commodities could be established, Africa would take a mighty step toward modernization. Money would come to the people, raising their standard of living and financing their education. A prosperous and educated people are impossible targets for slavers.

But how did the Zambezi River fit into all this? Trade routes, Livingstone knew, would be needed to bring the native goods out from the interior. The Zambezi, cutting east and west across the continent, might prove to be a splendid route.

The river had never been charted along its full length. It was known to empty into the Indian Ocean near the port of Quelimane, but no one had ever sailed it from there as far inland as the land of the Makololo. Nor had the Zambezi ever been traced from Makololo territory west to the Atlantic, if indeed the river ran that far. Livingstone's idea was to explore it both east and west. To the west, he would see if it finally broke into the Atlantic. To the east, he would see whether it was navigable for trading boats all the way to the Indian Ocean. With his other African travels behind him, Livingstone felt he was just the man for the job.

He sent his family to England in mid-1852 and returned by himself to the Zambezi, arriving at the Makololo town of Linyante in the spring of 1853. Livingstone elected to explore west first and, after performing a number of missionary chores, set out along the river with twenty-seven native helpers in November. Livingstone followed the Zambezi west for several weeks, only to see it curve north and become a small, disappearing stream in the mountains. It would never carry anyone to the Atlantic.

But perhaps an overland trade route could be forged from the point at which the Zambezi disappeared. Livingstone abandoned his boats and started to hike west through Portuguese Angola, beginning a journey that was to be the most difficult he had ever undertaken. He trudged through miles of sharp grass that cut his hands and legs. He forded rivers and felt their swift-flowing waters rise to his chest and threaten to pull his feet out from under him. He tried to see his way through torrential downpours. He entered swamps where sleepy-eyed crocodiles lay. He cut a path through jungles so dense that hardly a shaft of sunlight could reach him. Mosquitoes bit him until his face was swollen, red, and raw. His food ran low. He came down with fever and dysentery, and the pounds slipped away from his lean frame like water running down a steep bank. But somehow Livingstone kept moving, and somehow he mapped his every step and studied the geology and the plant and animal life that surrounded him.

On May 31, 1854, the journey ended at the Atlantic port of Loanda. Livingstone had covered more than fifteen hundred miles since departing Linyante, and he was now little more than a walking skeleton, the skin hanging loose on his

arms, his face gaunt, his step weak. He turned to his native
companions and forced a smile. They had come a great
distance, but now they must go back to Linyante and start
all over again, this time to look eastward. There was no
possible trade route to the west. The land of Angola would
defeat every goods wagon that dared come its way.

He lingered on the coast just long enough to regain some
of his strength and then, with his usual impatience to get on
with the job at hand, retraced his steps to Linyante. There
he prepared for the expedition eastward. And from there, in
November of 1855, he set out along the Zambezi. Traveling
with him now were two hundred natives in dugout canoes.

The first days were passed in heavy rains. The natives
looked worriedly at their missionary leader. They knew
that Livingstone had never fully recovered his health after
the Angola journey, and in the rainstorms he became soaked
to the skin and shivered violently. He seemed so frail, and
there were great streaks of gray in his hair and beard. Livingstone became aware of the natives' concern one night when
he awoke to find himself covered with an extra blanket. It
belonged to a Makololo chieftain, who had draped it over
Livingstone to protect him from the damp night air. It was
the only blanket that the man owned.

The sun finally broke out, though, and it was under clear
skies that Livingstone became the first white man to see one
of the most awesome sights that Africa has to offer—the
breathtaking Victoria Falls.

Long before departing Linyante, Livingstone had heard
the Makololos say that he would come to a waterfall a short
distance downriver. They called it *Mosi oa tunya*, meaning,
variously, "the smoke that thunders" or "smoke does sound
there," and the natives said that it was a wondrous, giant
thing to see. Livingstone hoped that they were exaggerating.

A great waterfall would stand as an insurmountable barrier to the passage of future trading boats along the Zambezi. If the waterfall were small, though, then perhaps goods could be easily portaged around it. Livingstone shrugged. He would have to wait and see.

Just two weeks after getting underway, the explorer came to the upper side of the falls. His heart began to sink when he was still five or six miles away, for even then he could hear the thunder and see the smoke-like cloud of water vapor that climbed high above the falls. The Makololos, he was forced to admit, had not been exaggerating. These falls would be a terrible barrier. There could be no doubt about *that*.

When Livingstone finally saw the falls, they took his breath away. The Zambezi was at its widest at this point—more than sixteen hundred eighty yards across—and it abruptly dropped out of sight all the way from shore to shore, leaving behind the deafening thunder and the rainbow-streaked cloud of water vapor that curled upward for two hundred feet. Small islands lay all about, thrusting up out of the river like green warts, and Livingstone went ashore at one that seemed to hang right out over the falls. He walked to the island's edge and stared down. His whole world turned into crashing, foaming water. Its unending roar seemed to get inside him and vibrate in all corners of his being. He had never seen anything like this in all his life.

Unlike other falls, such as America's Niagara, the water at Victoria Falls did not plunge into a wide basin. Rather, it fell into a great split in the earth. The Zambezi moved toward the split on one side, while plateau land stretched away to the horizon on the far side. The split itself, Livingstone reckoned, ranged from eighty feet wide at some points to about two hundred forty feet at others and cut its way into the earth for up to three hundred sixty feet. Into the split poured the river water, falling past sheer rock walls in some places, dropping between long outcroppings in others, and crashing against boulder formations in still others. Long before the water reached the bottom of the chasm, it lost itself beneath the boiling cloud of vapor. But far over to one side, Livingstone saw the water tumble and race out from beneath the cloud and then batter its way through a series of narrow gorges that finally opened into the riverbed that was the continuation of the Zambezi.

Livingstone later wrote that he stood rooted and "feasted my eyes long on the beautiful sight." But the beauty and the vibrating roar inside him could not blot out his disappointment. There would be no easy and inexpensive portage of goods past this barrier. There would be no trade route along the Zambezi all the way from the Indian Ocean to the heart of Africa. The trade route would end at this point.

Livingstone stayed that day and the next on the island, carved his initials and the date 1855 in a tree trunk to commemorate his visit, and christened the falls in honor of Britain's Queen Victoria. He wrote in his notebook that this marked the first time that he had ever given an English name to one of his African discoveries.

Then Livingstone and his followers worked their way down to the continuation of the Zambezi.

All that the explorer could hope for was that the river would be navigable up to the falls. That would be better than nothing.

But this hope was shattered weeks later when, little more than two hundred miles from the end of his journey, Livingstone came to the long stretch of wild water called the Quebrabasa Rapids. Dejectedly, knowing that his dream of a Zambezi trade route was now definitely ended, Livingstone hiked past the rapids and made his way to the Portuguese settlement of Tete. From there, he traveled overland to the Indian Ocean port of Quelimane, located a short distance to the north of the mouth of the Zambezi.

Livingstone was as thin and as weak as ever. It was May, 1856, and all that he could think was that he had spent two and a half years searching west and east on a mission that had ended in failure.

But the world refused to agree. Once they had heard of his travels, people everywhere recognized their value. Livingstone had made his way all across the width of Africa, a feat never before accomplished by a white man. He had charted the full length of a great and dangerous river. He had collected a mountain of information about Africa's people, its geology, and its plant and animal life. Livingstone had filled in the map of one of the continent's most mysterious areas. More than any man before him, people said, he had stripped away the darkness from the Dark Continent.

Livingstone returned to England at the close of 1856 to visit his family and to take a well-deserved and much-needed rest. There was ample time for visiting with his loved ones —he saw to that—but few precious moments for relaxation. Livingstone received a hero's welcome, gave a series of speeches on his adventures, and wrote a book titled *Missionary Travels and Researches in South Africa*.

In all his speeches and in his book, Livingstone spoke out sharply against the practice of slavery. Having found no trade route to the interior, he knew that he would never bring an end to slavery and that the world would have to wait for a more enlightened time before men found intolerable the idea of keeping their fellow men in bondage. The explorer could only hope that his words would hasten that time.

Refreshed and eager for more exploration, Livingstone went back to Africa in 1858. He did not travel alone as a medical missionary this time, but as the leader of a British expedition with government orders to continue the investigation of the Zambezi region. In a steam launch, Livingstone and his party sailed northward along the Shire River, a tributary of the Zambezi, until they were stopped by the Murchison Rapids. Livingstone then pushed farther north on foot until he reached the giant Lake Nyasa, becoming the first white man to visit its shores.

Once the work of the expedition was done, Livingstone made his way back to the land of the Makololo and spent his next years working there as a missionary. He interrupted his labors from time to time to return to Lake Nyasa. He explored its eastern shore and helped to establish the first Christian missions there. He was proud of his Nyasa accomplishments but heartbroken over one result that they brought. He who hated slavery with such a passion saw his mapping of the Nyasa region open that beautiful area to Portuguese slave traders.

Other heartbreak soon followed. In 1862, Livingstone's beloved Mary returned to Africa to assist him in his missionary work, but, only two months after her arrival, she fell ill with malaria and died. Her death almost crushed Livingstone. Hoping to forget his grief in work, he plunged into the wilderness to explore it and to bring medical help to its peoples. The years netted him the discoveries of Lake Tanganyika (to the northwest of Lake Nyasa) and the nearby lakes of Mweru and Bangweulu.

But the outside world heard little or nothing of these finds, for from 1866 to 1871, not a word came out of Africa of Livingstone's whereabouts. Africa seemed to have covered him over with her age-old darkness. People throughout the civilized world began to ask anxious questions. Where was Livingstone? Was he still alive?

The mystery held a particular appeal for American James Gordon Bennett, the owner of the *New York Herald* newspaper. In addition to a genuine desire to learn what had happened to the missionary, Bennett knew that, should he solve the mystery, he would capture the greatest news story of the century for his paper. And so it was that in 1870 he got in touch with writer Henry Morton Stanley and sent him off to Africa with one simple instruction: find Livingstone.

Stanley, he knew, was just the man for the job. Though the twenty-nine-year-old writer had never been to Africa, he was an adventurer to the core, more than willing to take on any assignment that promised danger and excitement. Born in Wales in 1841, Stanley had sailed to the United States as a young man and had won a reputation as a news reporter by traveling through and writing about the Far West. Later, his writing had taken him to Asia Minor and Tibet.

Stanley landed at Zanzibar on Africa's east coast in January, 1871. Accompanied by a large party of natives, he was soon pushing his way inland towards Lake Tanganyika. He had no idea where Livingstone might really be, but he was following a native rumor that said the missionary was now living at the tiny village of Ujiji at the northern end of the lake. If the rumor was to be believed, Livingstone had fallen ill some months earlier while traveling in the vicinity of Tanganyika and had been taken to the village to recover.

Stanley arrived at the lake in November of the year 1871 and made his way to Ujiji. There, he saw a gray-haired, gray-bearded man, so frail and thin and bent that he could hardly rise from his chair on the porch of a native hut and walk toward the newcomer. Stanley looked closely at the haggard face and recognized it from news photographs that he had studied. He smiled, extended his hand, and ended the mystery of David Livingstone's whereabouts with four words that were to become famous in the history of exploration: "Dr. Livingstone, I presume."

Stanley remained at Ujiji for four months and came to admire Livingstone more than any other man he had ever met. The veteran explorer described his recent years of African travel and told of how he had been carried to this village after falling prey to his old enemy, dysentery, some months earlier. Stanley nodded. The native rumors had been true in every detail. He implored the missionary to return to England, arguing that his health could no longer stand up to the rigors of the wilderness.

Livingstone shook off the warning with a smile. He could not go home, he said. Africa was his life. He had much work yet to do. When he had fallen ill, he had been in the midst of one of his most important explorations—the search for the source of the mighty Nile River. He must get on with it as soon as he was fit again.

Stanley saw the dark glow in his friend's eyes. He knew that further argument was useless.

The Ujiji visit ended on March 15, 1872, when the two men shook hands and bade each other farewell. Each was greatly changed as a result of the four months they had spent together. In that time, Livingstone had taught Stanley all that he knew of exploration and had taken him on map-making tours around Lake Tanganyika. Stanley was now under Africa's spell and was determined to explore the country on his own; ahead of him were years in the jungle, years that would climax with his charting of the Congo

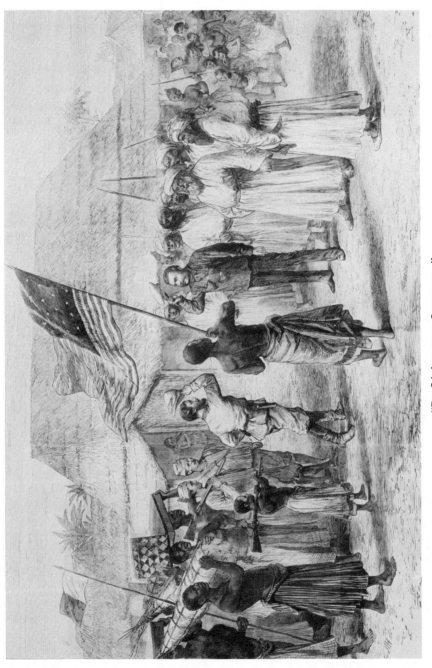

"Dr. Livingstone, I presume."

River. As for Livingstone, the visit had so invigorated him that he felt strong enough to get back to his hunt for the source of the Nile.

Though the Nile's source was found in the region of Lake Victoria by England's John Speke in the 1830s, Livingstone was obsessed with the idea that the source of the river was actually located far to the southwest of Lake Tanganyika, and it was in this direction that he headed in mid-1872. Soon, he found himself wading through the vast swamp just north of Lake Bangweulu. The swamp—with its murky, insect-laden waters—and the simple, coarse food of the expedition were dangerous enough to Livingstone's health, but the rainy season arrived to make matters even worse. His dysentery returned, immediately weakening him to the point where he could no longer travel.

Livingstone made his way to a sandy island in the swamp and rested at a tiny village there. His native bearers, always anxious about his frail health, were happy to see him begin to recover, but were aghast when, in just three weeks, he announced that he was ready to travel again. Livingstone needed many more weeks of rest and good goat's milk, the natives told one another. But who could convince him of *that*? He was a determined man, and always so impatient to be on his way.

Livingstone was too impatient. Into the swamp he again plunged, part of the time wading and part of the time riding in a canoe as he pushed his way south along the edge of Lake Bangweulu so that he could finally turn southwest toward the supposed area of the Nile's source. The waters were at flood stage from the heavy rains, and they battered him at his every step, soaking him through to the skin. His dysentery returned. He tried to ignore it, bending himself to his endless map making. But he grew weaker with each passing day. Finally, in early 1873, Livingstone could not stand, let alone walk. His bearers placed him on a litter and carried him to a village on the south side of the lake, arriving there on April 29.

Livingstone was put to bed in a thatched hut. The next day, he was so weak that he could barely manage to wind his watch. Outside, his native bearers sat in a silent circle, knowing that the end was at hand for the man they had long called the "great master." At dawn on May 1, two of the natives entered the hut. They found Livingstone kneeling alongside his bed. His heart had stopped beating sometime during the night.

A lifetime of travel—travel that had covered twenty-nine thousand miles—was finished. David Livingstone was dead at sixty years of age.

Silently and reverently, the natives embalmed his body and carried it all the way back to Zanzibar on the east coast, a journey of a thousand miles. From there the body was returned to London for burial at Westminster Abbey, the final resting place for England's greatest men.

But the natives, in their primitive wisdom, had made certain that something of their beloved missionary explorer remained in the land to which he had given such service. Prior to the final journey to Zanzibar, they had removed his heart and buried it close by the village where he had died.

Thus, they made Livingstone a part of the Africa that he had so loved, an Africa that was to beckon many explorers and settlers to its shores through the next years, an Africa that would slowly reveal its many secrets and would finally emerge from its age-old darkness.

Part Five

9

The Arctic

An invisible line girdles the forehead of our globe at 60°31′ north latitude, forming the Arctic Circle. Within the circle lie vast seas, great land masses, and rocky islands. The Arctic Ocean, all 5.4 million square miles of it, plunges to depths of up to eighteen thousand feet and is dotted with such islands as Spitzbergen, Novaya Zemlya, and the Franz Josef and New Siberian groups. The far northern Pacific Ocean, with its Aleutian Islands and its Bering Strait, is within the circle, as is the Atlantic with its Iceland and Faeroe Islands. And the uppermost reaches of North America, Greenland, Sweden, Norway, and Russia are included within the circle, giving the Arctic Ocean its barren coastline. All together, these lands and seas constitute one of the world's most inhospitable areas.

Ice chokes the Arctic Ocean all year long, releasing its grip on the fringes of the sea only for brief periods during the warmer months. Temperatures, though they can climb to eighty-five degrees during the summer in Alaska, spend most of their time below the zero mark and can spear down to eighty and ninety degrees below zero in certain areas. The Arctic year, thanks to the tilt of the earth's axis, divides itself sharply into two seasons—night and day. Darkness falls about the end of October and remains until sometime in March. Cold sunlight takes over for the rest of the time.

Forbidding and inhospitable though it may be, the Arctic has been the scene of much exploration during the past four hundred years. Earlier, the region was known only to the people who lived there—the Eskimos, the Lapplanders, the natives of Siberia, and the venturesome Vikings of Norway—and to a handful of travelers from the outside. We met the best known of those outsiders in the first section of this book—Pytheas of Greece, who made his way into far northern waters in 325 B.C., and the Irish monks, who, about twelve hundred years later, discovered the Faeroes and Iceland. But, in the sixteenth century, exploration of the Arctic began in earnest.

Why? For the very same reason that sent the Portuguese south to Africa's Cape of Good Hope and Columbus west across the Atlantic. Men still wanted to find new trade routes to the wealth of the Far East.

By the sixteenth century, merchants knew that they could reach the Far East along either of two sea lanes. They could sail along the Portuguese-blazed route around the Cape of Good Hope and thence east across the Indian Ocean, or they could drop down around the foot of South America and then beat their way northwest across the vast Pacific. The routes were known to all the trading nations of Europe, but to some they seemed quite beyond reach.

Spain had become the greatest sea power of the day, and Spanish policy dictated that the trade routes be open to none but Spanish vessels. Spanish captains harassed competing ships, sometimes boarding them and seizing their cargoes, sometimes delaying them in ports along the way while the goods in their holds rotted, and sometimes even sinking them. The small nations, such as England and the Netherlands, though smarting from such treatment, could do nothing to fight back. They just did not have the manpower and the ships to match the Spanish.

Yet England and the Netherlands wanted their share of the rich Oriental trade. They decided that they could solve the problem in but one way. They must establish trade routes of their own, routes that would be of no interest to Spain. They looked to the frozen Arctic for such routes.

Certain geographic beliefs of the day led England and the Netherlands to look in this direction. European scholars and map makers, now knowing for certain that the world was round, had developed the theory that Europe and the New World were actually vast islands. Since man could sail south of them, they reasoned, then he should also be able to sail north of them to make port in the Orient.

On the basis of this reasoning, England and the Netherlands concluded that there must be three northern trade routes—or passages—to the Orient. One must run eastward across the top of Sweden, Norway, and Russia to the Pacific; to this route, they gave the name the Northeast Passage. The second trade route, which they called the Northwest Passage, must pass across the top of Canada and Alaska. The third route was one that must pass directly over the North Pole and then drop south into the Pacific.

These routes sounded fine when scholars spoke of them, but sailing over them was quite another matter. A ship would have to venture into uncharted seas, jammed with ice and perhaps blocked by as-yet-undiscovered lands. The first job was to find the passages, to see if there was actually some sea path through all the ice to the Orient. It was a job for the explorers.

Beginning in 1553, England sent expeditions in search of the Northeast Passage. Men such as Hugh Willoughby, Richard Chancellor, and Charles Jackman sacrificed their lives to the quest. Willoughby and his crew were frozen to death while their ship lay locked in the ice at Kola Peninsula on the northern coast of Russia. Chancellor drowned when his ship went down in a storm off Scotland. Jackman sailed into the Arctic wastes and was never seen again.

Other Englishmen—among them Arthur Pet—escaped with their lives but reported that they had ranged far and wide above the Russian coast without finding a path through the icy waters.

The Dutch soon joined the British in the search. Chief among the Dutch explorers was the bearded Willem Barents. He made three voyages to the northeast—in 1594, 1595, and 1596. His last voyage, though it claimed his life, won him the honor of being the first European to live through the long Arctic winter night.

Barents rounded the northernmost tip of Norway and pushed eastward into icy seas in 1596. He reached the island of Novaya Zemlya, which lay across his path above Russia. He guided his ship around the northern tip of the island and saw that a great sea stretched away to the east for as far as he could see. But it was a sea jammed with ice.

That ice closed round Barents's ship and threatened to crush it. He took refuge in a small cove on Novaya Zemlya, for winter was now at hand, and there was not time to run for home. Barents called the cove Ice Haven and had his men build a cabin—complete with a bathtub made of a water barrel—from ship's timbers. The party stayed in the cabin throughout the winter, huddling about a fire while they shivered in thin clothes not meant for the harsh Arctic climate. They spent part of their time killing little foxes for food and for furs out of which they fashioned caps.

Only one man died during the long winter, but Barents himself fell ill and was near death by the spring. Because ice still blocked the cove, he was unable to free his ship, and so he led his men away in two small boats. They threaded their way south through ice floes and freezing winds to the Russian coast. Several days before they were rescued by a Russian fishing boat, Barents died and was buried at sea.

These many fruitless expeditions caused the British and the Dutch to abandon the search for the Northeast Passage. They were convinced that there was no navigable path through all the ice. It remained for Sweden's Baron Nils Nordenskjold to locate the passage—three long centuries later. In 1878, his steamship *Vega* worked its way eastward all along the Russian coast until it passed through the Bering Strait and into the Pacific. By this time, no one— including Nordenskjold himself—was interested in the Northeast Passage as a trade route. Nordenskjold undertook his journey simply to see if the passage was there at all.

England took the lead in searching for the second possible northern route—the Northwest Passage. In 1576, 1577, and 1578, Martin Frobisher set a northwestern course but managed to travel only as far as Frobisher Bay on what is now known as Baffin Island. Adventurers such as William Baffin, John Davis, and Robert Bylot followed Frobisher. They not only looked for the passage but also explored the west coast of Greenland and the vast expanse of Baffin Bay. On the western side of Baffin Bay, they encountered three large islands—Baffin, Devon, and Ellesmere—with straits running west between them. Beyond these straits, the adventurers found a welter of other islands, all of them now known as

Canada's Northwest Territorial Islands. Though they sailed
no farther, they theorized that, if a man could find a navigable path through the ice-choked waterways that ran among
the islands, he would finally break into the Pacific for an
obstacle-free run to the Orient.

England's search for the Northwest Passage centered
itself on these islands right up to the middle of the nineteenth century. Young Edward Parry sailed among them in
1819 and 1821 with Captain John Ross, who also made a
two-year voyage between 1829 and 1831. On that trip, the
captain's nephew, James Clark Ross, located the North Mag-
netic Pole on Boothia Peninsula, a point of land along the
northern Canadian coast.

The biggest single expedition to go in search of the
Northwest Passage was headed by Sir John Franklin. In
1845, he led two sturdy sailing ships—the *Terror* and *Erebus*
—and a company of 129 men in among the islands. Franklin
disappeared from sight for several years, and finally a string
of rescue parties was sent after him. All efforts to locate him
failed until 1859, when a note left by his men was found in
a little rock cairn on one of the islands—King William
Island.

The note told a sad story. In 1846, Franklin's ships had
become locked in the ice off King William Island and had
been slowly crushed during the next year and a half. The
long and terrible months had taken the lives of twenty-four
men, Franklin among them. The rest of the explorers had
set off across the ice in 1848, hoping to reach the Canadian
coast but disappearing into the Arctic wastes forever.

England closed its search for the Northwest Passage with
the Franklin expedition. Not only did the tragedy shock the
nation, but it also convinced everyone that the ice-choked
waterways running between the islands would always form

an impenetrable barrier for trading ships seeking the Pacific.

The opening years of the twentieth century saw Roald Amundsen of Norway demonstrate that the passage was navigable after all. Beginning in 1903, Amundsen voyaged among the islands, built a camp on King William Island, and remained there for two winters, making scientific studies of the region. Then he carefully poked his way through narrow channels until he broke into the Arctic Ocean along the Alaskan coast, sailing from there to the Pacific Ocean in 1906.

Though Amundsen proved that the passage was navigable, it shared the same fate as its sister path to the northeast. Commercial traders said that it would never serve as an efficient shipping route, for ice blocked it for too many months out of each year. There is presently, however, new interest in the passage, prompted by the existence of vast oil deposits in northern Alaska. The ship *Manhattan*, seeking to learn whether the passage could be used as a route for transporting oil to market, recently navigated the icy waters, though taking a route north of that forged by Amundsen. The future promises further experimental voyages.

The first attempts to reach the Orient via the North Pole were made in the sixteenth and seventeenth centuries. In 1527, two ships sailed north on orders from England's King Henry VIII and were never heard from again. Then, in the early 1600s, Henry Hudson attempted three voyages into the Arctic. He won the honor of discovering Hudson Bay on his third voyage but lost his life a short time later when his crew mutinied and set him adrift in a small boat with seven loyal followers. Hudson never made his way back to civilization.

Men soon realized that the North Pole is located in one

of the world's cruelest oceans. It is, they learned, a sea
covered over with a thick crust of ice—called ice pack—that
assumes many shapes. In some places, that crust is flat. In
other places, it is lined with sharp ridges created by the
wind's blowing ice particles into frozen heaps. In still other
places, the ice pack is a crazy-quilt of low mountains formed
of great ice blocks—called hummocks—piled one atop the
other. And in all places, the ice pack is constantly on the
move as the ocean current underneath sends it on an unending journey around the top of the world.

Learning all this, men admitted that the dream of a trade
route over the North Pole was an impossible one. But the
idea of the North Pole, located exactly at the crown of the
world, fascinated them. Here was a place where no one had
ever stood, a place that would demand the utmost of any
explorer who decided to reach it. The North Pole slowly
grew into one of the greatest prizes to be won in the history
of exploration. In the late nineteenth century, a handful of
adventurers began a contest to see who would be the first to
put this prize under his feet.

Among the first contestants was George Washington De
Long of the United States. In 1879, he sailed into the Arctic
Ocean via the Bering Strait, hoping that he would be able
to force his way through the ice to the North Pole. The
pack, however, caught him in its icy grip, held his ship
prisoner for two years, and finally crushed it. De Long lost
his life in the march of several hundred miles that his men
then made over the ice to the safety of the Russian coast.

Norway's great explorer, Fridtjof Nansen, fared better
in an 1893–1896 expedition. In a ship specially designed to
float atop the ice, Nansen allowed himself to be locked in the
pack with the hope that one particularly strong Arctic
Ocean current would see him drift up to the North Pole.

His ship came so close to its goal that he made a valiant but futile effort to sledge the rest of the way there.

The North Pole remained out of man's reach until early in the twentieth century. Then there appeared on the scene a bearded American explorer. His name: Robert Edwin Peary.

10

Robert Edwin Peary

Robert Edwin Peary was an American, but he looked like a tall Eskimo as he crawled from his igloo and gazed out at the ice-covered Arctic Ocean. He wore a coat of deerskin, trousers of bearskin, and boots of reindeer hide. His long face, highlighted by a sharp nose, heavy-lidded eyes, and a great beard, was circled by a halo of thick bear fur.

The time was 6:30 A.M. Peary stood on the northern shore of Ellesmere Island, which lies just to the west of Greenland. He knew that March 1, 1909, was to be one of the most memorable days in his life. In just a few moments, he was to launch another effort to reach the North Pole.

In all, Peary had attempted three expeditions in recent years to that long-sought-for stretch of ice called 90° North. Each expedition had failed, driven back by the vicious Arctic Ocean ice, the roaring winds, and the terrible cold. Now, at the age of fifty-two, Peary was going to try again. He realized that he *must* reach his goal this time. He would not be given another chance. He was getting too old for the hardships of Arctic exploration.

Nearby, more than a dozen sledges and their yapping, cavorting dog teams were strung out in a line along the shore. All were pointed toward the North Pole, 413 nautical miles across the ice. Standing alongside the sledges were four Americans and eleven Eskimos, each dressed, as was Peary, in about twenty-five pounds of fur. They were all moving in place, stamping their feet and swinging their arms to keep the blood circulating in the 50 degrees-below-zero cold.

Peary walked along the sledges, checking their lashings and cargoes. He nodded to the men as he walked, receiving smiles from the Eskimos and wind-whipped calls of "hello" from the Americans—Donald B. MacMillan, Ross Marvin, Dr. John Goodsell, and Matthew A. Henson.

The four Americans were lithe, muscular men. With the exception of Henson, they were in their twenties and thirties. Henson, a Negro, was forty years old and a veteran polar traveler. He had been Peary's assistant for eighteen years and had accompanied him on every one of his major explorations. Henson was an expert sledge driver and had learned to speak the Eskimo language like a native.

Peary slapped his gloved hands together with satisfaction at the end of his walk. Everything was in readiness. There was no point in delaying a moment longer. He raised his arm and pointed north. Instantly, the men sprang to their sledges and shouted the dog teams into straight, tugging lines. The sledges, each carrying twelve hundred pounds of supplies, jumped forward, their runners snapping free of the frozen ground. Henson's sledge took the lead. Peary stood to one side as the rigs jolted past him. Then he jumped aboard the last in line. Within minutes, the expedition was off the shore and onto the ice of the Arctic Ocean.

It seemed to Peary that he had been waiting for this

moment for most of his life. Born at Cresson, Pennsylvania, on May 6, 1856, he had grown up to become a naval engineer with the rank of commander in the U.S. Navy. But engineering had never been his major love—at least, not since the day in 1885 when he had read a magazine article on the Greenland icecap. From that moment, his interest in the Arctic had developed to the point where he decided to spend the rest of his working days in polar exploration. Peary had charted northwestern Greenland in the 1890s and then had looked out across the Arctic Ocean wastes towards the North Pole. In common with every great explorer before him, he found an all-consuming dream flowering inside him—the dream of reaching an impossible goal. Peary's particular dream? To be the first man in history to stand at the North Pole.

He had been trying to reach that goal for ten years. In 1899, Peary came to Ellesmere Island for the first time and established the camp that would serve as the headquarters for his expeditions. He made his first run north in 1900, his next in 1902, and his third in 1906. Each time he was turned back by the cruel weather. But each time Peary managed to struggle a little closer to his destination. Perhaps now, on his fourth try, he would succeed.

He knew that he had a good chance of success this time. Assisting him were some excellent men. Already, far ahead of him, were two helpers who had headed north a day early. One, a tough thirty-three-year-old seaman named Bob Bartlett, was hacking a path through the jumbled ice for him and establishing a string of campsites for his use. The other was George Borup, who was just twenty-one years old. He was dropping extra supplies at the campsites.

In all, Peary now had six Americans, seventeen Eskimos, 133 dogs, and nineteen sledges out on the ice. All were proceeding north according to a strict plan. It was a two-part plan that Peary had developed during his unsuccessful assaults on the North Pole.

The first part called for Peary's men to do most of the work on the trail—driving the dog teams forward and hauling the sledges over any and all obstacles—while he took life as easy as possible. At first glance, the idea appeared selfish on Peary's part, but it was grounded in hard experience. The terrible Arctic cold exhausted a man quickly, filled him with pain, and made him fatally dull-witted. Peary intended to guard against illness and fatigue at all costs. The first part of the plan would help him conserve his energies so that he could put them to use in those critical days when the North Pole was close at hand.

The second part of Peary's plan dictated that the *entire* expedition was not to reach the North Pole. Rather, the men and the sledges were to bring Peary as close to his destination as possible. As the sledges used up their food supplies, they would be returned to base camp in the charge of the men most tired at the time. At last, when the North Pole was just a few days' march ahead, Peary would send back the weakest of the remaining men. Only the strongest four or five men would accompany Peary on the final run.

It was a good plan, Peary knew, one that would insure him and his companions of the greatest strength at the very time when they most needed it. It *had* to be a good plan, he told himself, if it was to see him safely across 413 nautical miles of shifting Arctic Ocean ice pack.

Immediately, the Arctic Ocean showed Peary what it held in store for him. A sharp wind drove ice needles up off the pack and into the men's faces, blinding them. It turned the air so cold that brandy in a bottle tucked deep within the folds of Peary's clothing was frozen solid in a matter of minutes. He peered ahead and could not see the trail that Bartlett had cut just a few hours earlier. The ocean current had shifted it over out of sight, and the sledges, rather than bouncing along a prepared and relatively smooth trail, were being forced to climb over one ice hummock after another. Up at the head of the line, Henson's sledge got away from him and careened down the jagged face of a hummock. The sledge rolled over on the ice below, its lashings torn from its frame.

Henson crouched in the wind to make repairs. The other sledges—under orders not to stop except for the most dire emergencies—jolted past him. He glanced calmly at them, for he had no doubt that he could fix the rig and be on his way again quickly. On a previous expedition, he had built one complete sledge out of two smashed ones. All that concerned Henson now was the bitter cold. He had to take off his gloves to work, and, with the temperature at fifty degrees below zero, he could leave his bare hands exposed only for brief seconds before they began to freeze. And so the repair job was a stop-and-start one. Repeatedly, Henson jammed his hands up into his armpits and held them there until circulation returned.

No sooner had Henson overtaken Peary than he had to help repair another sledge, one that had been broken when it and its Eskimo driver tumbled back while climbing a hummock. Another sledge took such a fall that it split itself down the middle.

It seemed to Peary that every minute of that March 1 presented a new and maddening problem. Yet the party managed to cover a distance of ten miles before day's end, at last reaching a cluster of igloos built by trailblazer Bob Bartlett. The men fed their dog teams and then crawled inside the igloos for a meal of pemmican, a treated meat-and-

Robert Edwin Peary

Matthew A. Henson

fat compound originally developed by the North American
Indians and used by Peary on all his expeditions because
it was easy to carry and highly nutritious. The men were
dead tired, but they faced a sleepless night. To keep from
freezing to death, they spent the time moving about as best
they could in their cramped quarters and beating their arms
and bodies.

The second day's march began at dawn and, almost immediately, brought a scowl to Peary's face. On the northern
horizon, a great cloud seemed to be swirling right up from
the ice. Peary knew it for what it was—a vapor cloud. It
signaled that the ice pack was broken somewhere ahead and
that open water lay in his path. The cloud was caused by
the water's steaming in the cold air.

Open water in the ice is called a lead. In Peary's estimation, a lead was among the most dreaded obstacles that he
could encounter. To save weight, he did not carry any boats
and so could not paddle directly across it. If the lead were
wide and if he could not work his way around it, he might
be stalled for hours or even days on end. And if the ice
refused to close over at all, it could keep Peary from reaching
his goal.

At a little past four in the afternoon, with a seven-mile
hike behind him, Peary reached the lead. The break in the
ice was a quarter of a mile wide from south to north, and it
sprawled across his path for as far as the eye could see from
east to west. He viewed the steaming black water first with
alarm and then with fury. He shuddered as he wondered
whether the lead had opened after Bartlett and Borup were
safely past or had split directly beneath them and plunged
them to their deaths. Hot anger came when he explored
along its length and saw that it stretched so far away to the
east and west that there was no possibility of traveling

around it. He would just have to sit here and lose precious time while waiting for the ice on either side to shift back together again.

Peary and his men built four igloos and fed their dogs. While Peary was settling down to his own dinner, he heard an alarmed shout from the direction of the lead. He looked up to see MacMillan and Ross Marvin running toward the igloos; MacMillan's clothes were drenched and stiffening with icy water. In the next moments, Peary learned what had happened. The two young men had sledged over to the lead and had dropped a line into the ocean to measure its depth, but the ice underfoot had given way, and MacMillan had dropped into the water. He had caught the back of the sledge and had hung on until pulled to safety by Marvin. Peary hurried him into one of the igloos and helped him pull off his frozen clothing. Then, while MacMillan tugged his way into fresh clothes, Peary held the man's icy feet against the warmth of his own chest.

The men bedded down for an uncomfortable night, but at five o'clock the next morning—March 3—all their discomfort was forgotten. They awoke to a deafening sound outside, a sound like that of a hundred cannons going off. To Peary and his men, it was the most welcome sound in the world, for it was the crash and grind of the ice to either side of the lead coming together and closing it over. The men dashed outside, got their dogs into harness, and watched the stretch of black water grow narrower by the minute. At last, when the stretch of water was only a few feet wide it began to freeze, creating a filmlike bridge between the two moving ice masses. Immediately, Peary waved the men forward, and they took the sledges across the disappearing lead at a dead run. The ice underfoot was so thin that they felt it undulating, just as if it were water. They kept their feet wide apart to reduce the concentration of their weight and slid them along so as not to poke any holes in the frail surface.

No sooner had he reached the far side of the lead than Peary felt his luck change. He found the ice here flat to the horizon, promising a smooth journey, at least for the time being. He came upon Bartlett's trail and sighed with relief; the lead had not claimed the trailblazer's life. The wind died and the temperature rose to twenty degrees below zero, bringing weather that seemed balmy when compared to that of the past days. The miles fell quickly away from under the sledges all through the days of March 3 and 4.

But March 4 ended in discouragement. A new vapor cloud swirled into view, climbing high into the sunless sky, and at mid-afternoon Peary came up to a lead that made a dwarf of the one farther south. In front of him was an expanse of water that stretched at least half a mile over to its northern shore, while disappearing out of sight to the east and west. Peary found Bob Bartlett and his companion parked on the lead's southern side. The two men shook hands and then, as one, turned grim eyes on the steaming water. Bartlett muttered that he had arrived here two days ago. The lead had given no indication of closing in all that time.

Peary groaned inwardly. Two days! How long, he wondered, would he be stalled here? Peary was trapped for almost seven days. He watched the men and dogs consume precious supplies. He glowered at the weather because it was perfect for travel, and he added up all the miles that he could be putting behind him, were it not for the lead. He tried not to think that the lead might keep him from reaching his goal on this, his fourth and last try for the North Pole. He watched the Eskimos, all of them superstitious to the core, grow nervous and say that the evil spirit *Tornasuk* had put the lead in their path because, for some reason, he was angry with the expedition. The Eskimos began to talk of turning back for home.

Twenty-two-year-old Donald MacMillan emerged as Peary's most valued helpmate during these trying days. MacMillan, by nature pleasant and enthusiastic, loved the Arctic and was fascinated by all that he saw in this barren, white world. He immediately took the frightened Eskimos in hand and kept them busy with an unending string of games, games that delighted the simple and primitive men. He organized boxing and wrestling matches—and even contests in thumb-pulling. An astonished Peary heard him announce the prizes to be given to the winners of the bouts. Happily, MacMillan awarded such items as the anchor, keel, and spars from the ship that had transported the expedition from the United States.

The lead started to close on March 9, finishing the job two days later. Peary hurried the sledges across and immediately recalled the smooth pack on the southern side with affection, for now he found the ice in chaos. There were hummocks pushed against each other. There were sharp ridges where ice crystals had been blown into frozen piles by the wind. There were great blocks of ice tossed up one atop the other. Henson took over the job of trailblazing from Bob Bartlett. The next days became a nightmare of backbreaking work for him and his two Eskimo helpers.

Patiently, the three men chipped a path through the low ice ridges. Whenever they came to hummocks or crazy castles built of ice blocks, they searched for a path around them. If they found none, they hacked a trail or a series of footholds up over the top of the obstacles, at times requiring two hours to get the job done. Then they dragged or lifted their sledge up to the peak and lowered it down the far side, signaling for the rest of the expedition to follow them. Despite the cold, they were bathed in perspiration.

To make matters worse, the ice underfoot was crisscrossed with deep fissures. Covered over with snow, the fissures were perfect traps, and time and again, Henson's dog team blundered into them. Henson and his Eskimos sometimes hauled the dogs out by pulling hand over hand on their traces. More often, they leaned far down into the fissures and lifted the struggling animals out bodily.

Yet, despite the hardships of the trail, the expedition reached 84°29′ north latitude by March 14, the farthest north that man had ever traveled in this world. Peary decided that the time had come to begin sending the weakest of the men back to base camp. Dr. John Goodsell was the first to go, followed a day later by Donald MacMillan, who was now suffering from a frozen heel. Young George Borup went on March 20, and Ross Marvin on March 25. Each was accompanied by two or three Eskimos. All but Marvin reached camp safely.

Tragedy overtook Marvin less than a week after he left Peary. It struck when, in the company of two Eskimos named Kudlookto and Inuygeeto, Marvin encountered an area of thin ice crisscrossed with tiny leads and pools of open water.

As Kudlookto later told Peary, he warned Marvin to be careful of the ice when the young explorer decided to scout ahead for danger spots. Marvin nodded, said that he would keep his eyes open, and hurried out of sight. Kudlookto and Inuygeeto followed his footprints and suddenly came upon a spot where the ice was broken into small pieces and a mist was steaming up from the exposed water.

The two Eskimos stared in horror. Floating there in the steaming water, with his face down and his coat filled with air, was Marvin. It was obvious that the young man had fallen through the ice and then had smashed the surrounding ice in an effort to struggle out. The freezing water had taken his life in seconds.

The sight of the dead man terrified the two Eskimos, for they were certain that evil spirits had killed him. It was a belief of their people that, when a man dies, he goes right on with his work in the hereafter, and so they fetched his belongings from the sledge and set them alongside him. Then they built an igloo and, still frightened that evil spirits were lurking nearby, huddled in it throughout the night. By morning, the broken ice was healed over. Marvin was gone.

Far to the north, Peary and his men, unaware of the tragedy, were working their way through one obstacle after another. One day, a sledge was smashed to bits when it got away from its Eskimo handlers as they were lowering it down the face of a thirty-foot hummock. On another occasion, a dog was killed when he fell into a fissure and a sledge crashed down on top of him. On still another day, as Henson was crossing a narrow lead jammed with floating blocks of ice, he lost his footing and plunged into the water. One of his Eskimo drivers, Ootah, came jumping from one ice block to another, reached down, and hauled Henson to safety.

By March 28, Peary reached a point just 180 nautical miles from the North Pole. He had covered more than half of the distance to his goal, closer than he had ever come before. But he ended the day's march with an angry scowl, for, once again, he found his path blocked by a stretch of open, steaming water.

The men built igloos for the night, with Bob Bartlett and his Eskimos choosing a spot about one hundred yards from the rest of the party. The Americans and Eskimos, after a quick meal of pemmican and hot tea, crawled into their igloos, grateful to lie down even in icy sleeping bags. They had no idea that one of the worst experiences of the trip would mark the opening of the next day.

A thundering sound woke the men at dawn. For a moment, Peary thought that the lead was closing, with the ice to either side of it crashing together. He rushed outside and stared aghast at his surroundings. The lead was not closing at all. Rather, a heavy wind had set the water into a violent motion that was disturbing the ice all about. The campsite was shuddering and heaving, just as if it were a ship being pounded by a stormy sea. Nearby hummocks, grinding and crashing, were on the move, advancing on the igloos and pressing against each other and sometimes piling one atop the other as they came. A sharp, cracking sound burst from underfoot, and Peary saw the flat ice around him begin to split in all directions. Fur-clad figures dashed by as the men ran to their dogs and lashed them to the sledges, eager to move away from danger.

Peary stepped after them but then stopped and watched a great crack come snaking northward along the ice between his cluster of igloos and those of Bartlett in the distance. Steaming water hissed up through the crack as it widened and zigzagged its way to the lead. Another movement caught his eye. He saw Bartlett crawl from his igloo. Excited Eskimos gathered about the little seaman and pointed wildly at the crack. The panel of ice under Bartlett's igloos began to move. The crack and the jolting movement of the nearby hummocks had broken it free of the pack.

The panel drifted out into the lead and swung toward Peary. Bartlett and his Eskimos were running to their sledges, pulling their dogs into harness, driving the rigs to the edge of the panel. Peary hurried over to the lead. Gathering speed in the icy current, the panel bore down on him. He knew that if it floated past it would carry Bartlett and his men off into the Arctic wastes, perhaps never to be seen again.

Eyes narrowed against the freezing wind, Peary watched the panel, rocking and dipping, sweep closer and closer. He saw that it was going to miss the ice on which he stood—but just by inches. Bartlett's sledges were now crowded up to its edge. All eyes were on the narrowing gap between the two sections of ice. At last the panel was directly opposite, brushing against the ice under Peary's feet and showering him with tiny particles of white. Bartlett yelled at his dogs, and they shot forward, yanking the sledges across to Peary. Bartlett and the Eskimos came leaping after them. The men then turned, as one, to watch the panel swirl away along the lead, finally carrying its cargo of igloos out of sight.

In the next days, it seemed to Peary that the adventure with Bartlett marked the last great obstacle that the Arctic Ocean threw up in his path. The lead closed on March 30, and the expedition crossed over to find itself a short time later on relatively smooth ice. On March 30, the sledges advanced twenty miles north, coming almost to 87°46′49″ north latitude, approximately one hundred thirty-three nautical miles from the North Pole.

April 1 saw Peary send Bob Bartlett and the weakest of the remaining Eskimos back to base camp. Remaining with Peary now were four Eskimos and the always-hardy Matthew Henson. Of the Eskimos, three had accompanied Peary on previous North Pole trips. They were Seegloo, Ootah, and Egingwah. The fourth was Ooqueah, a tireless, ambitious youngster. He hoped that the valor he showed in traveling with Peary would earn him the love of a young lady named Anadore back in his home village.

The men spent April 1 repairing their gear and readying

themselves for the final thrust north. They headed out with five sledges and forty dogs on April 2, moving so quickly over the hard, flat ice that, according to Henson's figuring, they covered almost twenty-five miles in ten hours.

On April 4, they encountered a lead, but one that was well frozen over. It ran north, and they followed it through that day and the next as though it were a highway, averaging more than twenty miles per march. Helping them along was the weather. The sky was overcast, but the wind had fallen off, and the temperature was up to a moderate fifteen degrees below zero.

Those two days were the most thrilling of Peary's life. He knew that he was walking where no man before had walked. Deep in his bones, he felt that nothing now could keep him from reaching his goal. Whenever he stared ahead, he tried to imagine that he was already at the North Pole.

At the close of April 5, Peary made a solar sighting with his sextant and jubilantly announced that the expedition had reached 89°25′ north latitude, a scant thirty-five nautical miles from the North Pole. Peary was so certain that success lay within his grasp after all the years of struggle that he could not sleep. He ordered the men back to the march at midnight. The sledges hurried forward, coming at last to a halt at ten o'clock in the morning of April 6.

Peary directed the Eskimos to build igloos. Then he walked to his sledge and removed from it a small package. Henson, watching, knew that they had come to journey's end. He had seen the package often in all his years with the explorer. It held a small taffeta flag that Peary always flew at the last camp reached in his expeditions.

Peary fastened the little flag to a staff that he then thrust into the dome of his igloo. He stepped back and watched it proudly. Henson later wrote that the little flag hung limp in the dead, still air for a moment. Then a small breeze arose out of nowhere and unfurled its bright colors against the background of unending white.

A solar observation showed the latitude to be 89°57'11" north. The expedition stood approximately three nautical miles from the North Pole. Peary slept for four hours and then began a work that he had long dreamed of doing. He hiked north twice, making solar observations as he went, thus establishing with absolute certainty that he passed directly over the North Pole. One observation showed that he had walked six miles beyond it. There could be no doubt that he had attained the "roof of the world."

Now only ceremony remained. Peary unfurled the American flag and allowed it to flutter over the ice. He photographed his men. He inserted two messages into a glass jar and placed the jar in the snow. One message claimed that the expedition owed its success to the organization that had financed it—the Peary Arctic Club of New York City. The other read:

> 90 N. Lat., North Pole
> April 6, 1909
> I have today hoisted the national ensign of the United States at this place, which my observations indicate to be the North Polar axis of the earth, and have formally taken possession of the entire region, and adjacent, for and in the name of the President of the United States of America.
> I leave this record and United States flag in possession.
> Robert E. Peary
> United States Navy

Then, at 4 P.M., April 7, 1909, Peary turned southward for home. The North Pole was conquered. The dream of his life was now a reality.

Part Six

11

The Antarctic

For more than a century, since man first sighted it, the giant land of Antarctica has been known as the White Continent. Blanketed the year round with a layer of ice that is two miles thick in some places, it is a mountainous continent of 5 million square miles at the bottom of the world. Three oceans—the Atlantic, the Pacific, and the Indian—surround it. The South Pole lies deep in its interior on a vast plateau ten thousand feet above sea level.

The Antarctic is a far more hostile place than its sister polar region to the north, the Arctic. It is reached by crossing seas torn by winds said to be the fiercest in the world. It is a land of such cold—its temperatures averaging ten degrees lower than those of the Arctic—that it can boast of no vegetation or human life. The only animals able to survive the Antarctic are the penguin, a small wingless fly, and a tiny spider. The penguin, with its black coat and strutting walk, was on hand to greet the first visitors to the continent in the nineteenth century. The wingless fly and the tiny spider are discoveries of our own century, found by scientist-explorers. These insects come alive only during the summer months, sleeping frozen in the ice for the rest of the year.

Scientists believe that Antarctica was not always the cold and forbidding continent that it is today. The geologic findings of recent years have convinced them that, millions of years ago, it was a warm land, a land of forests and swamps, a land teeming with primeval animals, among them the mighty dinosaur. Leading the scientists to this certainty have been the discoveries of fossil deposits, coal deposits, and the imprints of prehistoric leaves in the ice.

But, eons ago, the climate of Antarctica changed. The warmth disappeared and was replaced by an unspeakable cold. Many of the birds and animals escaped across the seas to warmer lands. Others, unable to fly or swim, perished and were sealed in an icy tomb. Only the penguin, the wingless fly, and the tiny spider managed to survive—the penguin due to his cold-blooded reptilian ancestry, and the fly and the spider due to their ability to remain alive when frozen.

In common with the Arctic, the Antarctic has fascinated men since earliest times. The ancient Greeks, as we have seen, theorized that there must be a great land mass at the bottom of the world to keep the globe in balance against all the heavy lands and winds to the north, adding the guess— one that was several million years off the mark—that it was a warm land covered over with thick and rich vegetation. In time, their imagined land became Terra Australis, the mythical continent that explorers from the sixteenth through the eighteenth century steadily reduced to the islands of the South Pacific.

By 1772, little remained of Terra Australis. But the region around the South Pole still remained unexplored. And so England decided to see if any of the old Terra

Australis could be found there. Captain James Cook, just returned from his first triumphant voyage to the South Pacific, was put in charge of two ships and sent down beyond the tip of South America and into a world of raging seas and howling winds. For close to two years, Cook poked his way around the bottom of the world. He threaded his way among towering icebergs. He lay blind for long days in dense fogs and watched sudden storms freeze his sails and rigging. He struggled constantly to keep the sea ice from pressing against his ships and crushing them. Cook sighted much marine life—whales, seals, octopuses, and jellyfish. He searched the horizon tirelessly and in vain for some glimpse of land. And he sailed farther south than any man before him.

England had hoped that Cook would return home with the news that he had found a continent that could be settled and developed and that could provide a treasure house of natural resources. But all that the captain could report was that he had failed to sight any sort of great land mass. There was, he felt certain, no Antarctic continent at all. The ancient Greeks and all their theories had been totally incorrect.

But, he added, he had discovered quite another treasure—the whale and seal colonies that abounded in the Antarctic waters. Here was a natural resource that could bestow untold wealth on England. England nodded and immediately sent fishermen south to mine the seas. Soon they were joined by eager competitors from other nations. Particularly sought after for its valuable pelt was the fur seal.

The next years saw the southern seas transformed from icy wastes into an efficient slaughterhouse, with sails on the horizon always signifying the arrival of death. So many of the fur seals were killed that their breed was soon threatened with extinction. But, greedy and busy though the seal hunters were, they performed a great service for exploration. It was they who, while nosing out new hunting grounds, took time to chart the Antarctic seas and finally sighted the giant continent that lay beneath a blanket of glittering ice.

England claims that, in 1820, seal hunter Edward Bransfield made man's first sighting of the continent, glimpsing what was later called Palmer Peninsula but is now known as the Antarctic Peninsula, a bent finger of land jutting out from the South American side of Antarctica. Russia says that Fabian von Bellingshausen sighted the peninsula a year earlier, while America argues that an American sealing skipper, young Nathaniel Palmer, deserves the honor of the first sighting, having come upon the peninsula in 1820 or 1821. The debate has never been settled—and likely never will be.

Though the three nations bickered over the first sighting, there was no longer any doubt that the continent actually existed. The ancient Greeks were avenged for Cook's unkind words. In the next years, Antarctica was glimpsed time and again by whalers, seal hunters, and then explorers. Among the whalers and sealers were England's James Weddell, John Biscoe, and Peter Kemp, and Norway's C. A. Larsen and Carsten Borchgrevink. Included in the ranks of the explorers were Jules S. C. Dumont d'Urville of France, James Clark Ross of England, and Charles Wilkes of the United States. All of them sailed along vast stretches of the Antarctic coast and mapped what they saw. Slowly, thanks to their efforts, the continent took shape in the eyes of the world.

The explorers' accomplishments and discoveries were many. Whaler Larsen, in 1894, managed to get so close to

Palmer Peninsula that he was able to go ashore and become the first man ever to set foot on the frozen continent. Five years later, Borchgrevink landed at a spot called Cape Adare, built a camp there, and spent man's first winter on the continent. And, long before either Larsen or Borchgrevink was born, Ross, an Englishman, discovered one of Antarctica's greatest natural wonders.

In 1840, while cruising along the Pacific side of Antarctica, Ross came upon a towering cliff of ice. Perfectly flat on top, it stretches far out to sea from the continent itself and extends for more than three hundred fifty miles along the coastline. The cliff has been formed through countless centuries by ice moving down glaciers from the continental mountains and has grown to the size of France. It rises to heights of two hundred feet above the sea and plunges below the surface of the water to depths of one thousand feet. It is today called the Ross Ice Shelf, in honor of its discoverer, and it has played a vital role in the Antarctic exploration of this century, for it offers one of the shortest passages from the sea to the South Pole. The distance from the outer edge of the shelf to the South Pole, deep inland, is approximately eight hundred miles.

The twentieth century brought a new breed of man to Antarctica. He was neither sealer nor whaler. He was not so much interested in charting the coast of the continent as he was in sledging far inland. Like Peary, far to the north in the Arctic, this new breed of man had one major goal in mind. He wanted to be the first to reach the South Pole.

Early in the century, two men of this new breed arrived in the Antarctic. Both gazed south, and the stage was set for one of the greatest—and most tragic—races in the history of exploration.

12

Amundsen and Scott

THE VAST ROSS ICE SHELF bustled with activity and excitement during the closing months of 1911. Two large expeditions, camped about three hundred fifty miles apart, were making final preparations for a race to the South Pole.

Heading the expeditions were Roald Amundsen of Norway and Robert Falcon Scott of England. Amundsen had his base at the Bay of Whales, a large indentation in the ice at the eastern end of the shelf. Scott was headquartered at McMurdo Sound, a body of water that came up to the shelf at its western end.

The two competitors bore little similarity to each other in physical appearance and temperament. The thirty-nine-year-old Amundsen was a jovial, outgoing man, tall and fair of hair and skin. He had been an explorer for all of his adult life and had loved every minute of it, thriving on the adventure and the hardship. Scott was forty-one years old, a quiet, studious man. He was dark-haired and of medium height.

By far, Amundsen was the more experienced polar explorer. He had first visited Antarctica in 1898, when Adrien de Gerlache of Belgium had sailed the steamship *Belgica* up close to Palmer Peninsula for the purpose of charting the many islands clustered off its coast. Ice had closed round the ship, trapped it, and held it prisoner for eleven months while the crew—including de Gerlache—fell prey to scurvy. Amundsen took command, first nursing the crew back to health and then dynamiting the vessel free of its frozen prison. Afterward, he headed into the Arctic and proved the Northwest Passage to be navigable by sailing through it between 1903 and 1906. In 1909, he went north again, this time intending to become the first man to reach the North Pole. When Amundsen learned that Robert Peary had beaten him to the punch there, he swung his eyes back to Antarctica—to the South Pole.

Scott, on the other hand, was a relative newcomer to polar exploration. A commander in the Royal Navy, he had become interested in the Antarctic in 1900 and had made his first trip there in 1902. He had performed a number of scientific studies on the Ross Ice Shelf and had attempted a run for the South Pole, only to have illness among his men stop him far short of his goal. Scott was back for his second try.

The two men shared one trait in common—an intense desire to be the first man to stand at the South Pole. Each knew of the other's ambition. Each knew of the other's presence on the glittering Ross Ice Shelf. Each knew that he was competing in one of the greatest races in the history of exploration.

The cheers of camp workers echoed in the freezing air on October 19, 1911, as Amundsen led four men, four heavily laden sledges, and fifty-two dogs out from the Bay of Whales

and faced south across the Ross Ice Shelf. He glanced back
to see pennants fluttering in a farewell salute from the rigging of his ship, parked in the bay.

Amundsen was a man of mixed feelings that day. On the
one hand, his spirits ran high. He was done with all the
weeks of preparation. The great adventure was starting.
Ahead lay some seven hundred miles of challenge, with the
South Pole looming at journey's end. With him were four
fine men—Svere Hassel, Oscar Wisting, Helmer Hanssen,
and Olav Bjaaland. They were all young—in their twenties
and thirties—all strong, perennially cheerful, and calm in
the face of crisis. He could not have asked for better traveling companions.

But Amundsen was also troubled. Worrisome questions
nagged his mind. Was Scott already on his way south? If so,
how far ahead was he in the race? Amundsen shrugged and
stared into the wind. There was no use fretting over such
questions. Time, and nothing else, would give him the
answers.

The first hours on the shelf passed smoothly, with the
sledges fairly skimming over hard, flat ice. Amundsen grin-
ned. If only things could go this way for the whole trip, he
would have no trouble at all in beating Scott. But he knew
that the shelf would not treat him kindly for long. There
would be trouble—soon.

There was trouble—and it came without warning, her-
alded only by a deafening crash as a wide strip of ice to one
side of the sledges gave way and revealed a yawning abyss.
The men were startled but neither surprised nor frightened.
With Amundsen, they had spent many a day on the shelf in
the past weeks laying down supply caches for the South Pole
run, and they had learned that the surface in this area was
deceiving. It looked hard and firm, but in reality it was

Roald Amundsen

nothing more than a thin covering for deep chasms that crisscrossed the shelf in all directions.

Now, as they plunged ahead, the men watched the surface give way on all sides every few moments. Once it collapsed on both sides of the sledges, and they found themselves swinging along a narrow ridge between two gaping holes. On another occasion, the ice gave way directly under Helmer Hanssen's sledge. He jumped to the head of his team, grabbed the lead dog's harness, and pulled hard. His strength and the scrambling of the dogs yanked the sledge to safety just as it was dropping from sight. A short time later, Olav Bjaaland's sledge ran into the same problem but failed to share in Hanssen's good luck.

As Hanssen had done, Bjaaland lunged for the lead dog's harness when the rig started to fall through a sudden cloud of ice and snow. But he could not move fast enough. With the dogs clawing at the icy surface to keep from being pulled in after it, the sledge ended up hanging and swinging to and fro in an abyss that seemed to have no bottom.

Weighted with about a thousand pounds of supplies, the sledge proved too heavy to be hand-hauled back to the surface. Amundsen said that, if the sledge was to be freed, someone would have to drop down into the abyss and unload it. As Amundsen spoke, he looked directly at Oscar Wisting, the smallest man in the group. Wisting sighed. raised his arms, and allowed a rope to be knotted about his middle. Strong hands lowered him into the abyss and held him in place while he transferred supply crates to ropes so that they could be raised to the surface. At one point, Wisting calmly called up the news that the chasm arched in under the ice on which his friends stood. Only a few feet of glistening, blue-white ice separated them from a fatal plunge.

Despite all the hazards, Amundsen arrived at his first supply dump—at 80° south latitude—in four days. He pushed
on to the second cache immediately, reaching it in early
November. He now stood at 82° south latitude, approximately two hundred twenty miles from the Bay of Whales.

Ahead, in the far distance, the mountains of the continent glittered in the chill sunlight. Amundsen gazed at
them hopefully. Glaciers descended from the mountains
all along the Antarctic coast, each sending an icy flow down
to the shelf. If luck were with him he would come upon a
glacier that he could follow like a highway up through those
mountains toward the high central plateau where the South
Pole was thought to lie. But should a glacier not be near at
hand he would be forced to climb over the very peaks themselves in search of the plateau. It would be a long, slow
process—one that might well cost him so much time that
he would lose the race.

At mid-month, when Amundsen came off the shelf, he
knew that, indeed, luck was with him. Looking like a giant
fall of white hair, a glacier came down from between two
mountain towers to his very feet. The climb along its sometimes smooth, sometimes rippled, and sometimes broken
length promised to be anything but a Sunday stroll, he
thought. But it was certainly more inviting than the rugged,
ice-paneled walls to either side. And it rose so high that it
might well open directly onto the central plateau itself. That
would be the luckiest stroke of all.

Without hesitation, the men flung themselves onto the
glacier. It rose steep and slick, and, repeatedly, the dog teams
slipped or stumbled on its surface and went sliding back
downhill for several feet or yards before Norwegian arms
could yank them to a halt. Yet for the next days, the climb
went well, without delay due to accident or injury.

Then what seemed to be an unending series of problems began near the summit. First, the party encountered a stretch of broken, twisted ice, caused by the flows of several minor glaciers into the main one. The men literally had to lift the sledges and the dogs up over the broken ice to the smooth summit above. The work was so strenuous that they shook themselves out of their fur jackets and rolled up their shirt sleeves. Even then, with the temperature far below the zero line, they were soaked with perspiration.

Then, on reaching the summit, they were stalled in their tents for five days by a sudden blizzard. But the worst stroke came when they were ready to travel again. Amundsen saw that he had not yet reached the central plateau. Instead of level ice stretching away south, one small valley and gorge after another lay ahead, one seeming to flow right out of the other, each rising a little higher than the preceding one. Amundsen shook his head and said that a long climb to the plateau still remained.

Slowly now, he led the way southward. Sometimes he picked his way through valleys cluttered with broken and upended ice. Sometimes he scaled icy walls. Sometimes he threaded his way around deep crevasses. Sometimes he floundered through waist-deep snow. Day and night, Amundsen was plagued with worry. Would he ever work his way out of this cluttered maze to the central plateau?

But on December 7—fifty-eight days after leaving the Bay of Whales—he broke free of the valleys and found himself on a high plateau that stretched away for mile after flat mile to the south. He took a solar reading and happily announced its results: 88° 16′ south latitude. He was now within one hundred miles of the South Pole. This had to be the central plateau. No more mountains or glaciers lay before him.

The preceding days had exhausted the group. Their clothing was worn, even ripped, from the sharp ice in the valleys just passed. Their faces were puffed and raw from the icy air. Their lungs burned with the effort of breathing at an altitude of ten thousand feet. But not one of them gave a thought to resting, invigorated as they were by the fact that they had come so close to their destination. They pushed their sledges ahead as fast as possible, shouting happily at their dogs as they went.

Only their eyes were troubled. Constantly, they searched the flat snow and ice ahead, searched for some sign of Scott, some fearful evidence to show that he had arrived there ahead of them.

On November 3, 1911, camp workers gathered to watch Commander Robert Falcon Scott depart on the first leg of his journey to the South Pole.

Cheers were again heard on the Ross Ice Shelf, this time echoing across the still waters of McMurdo Sound. Scott and his companions stood assembled for a final photograph and then hurried to their sledges. In another moment, they were on their way.

Scott's feelings exactly matched those of Amundsen sixteen days earlier at the Bay of Whales. Scott, too, was relieved that the long period of preparation was at last behind him. He, too, was eager for the journey ahead and for the goal that lay at its end. And he, too, was worried, wondering whether his competitor was already well on the way to the South Pole.

But there the similarity between the two ended. When compared with Amundsen's party, Scott's party resembled an army. Under Scott's command were thirteen sledges, sixteen men, two dog teams, eight Manchurian ponies, and two small, motorized tractors. The dog teams pulled two of the sledges, while the ponies and tractors took care of the rest.

The ponies—tough, shaggy little fellows—and the tractors had been introduced into the Antarctic by fellow British explorer Ernest Shackleton, who had accompanied Scott on his 1902 expedition and had himself once made an unsuccessful attempt to reach the South Pole. Shackleton believed that the ponies, stolid and quiet by nature, were easier to handle than excitable, yapping dogs. And he was convinced that motorized equipment was destined to play a vital role in future polar exploration. Scott agreed with Shackleton and was putting both beliefs to the test. As matters turned out, both the ponies and the tractors did little but get in the way.

In the main, the first days of the trip were pleasant and encouraging ones. Only the motorized tractors caused trouble. They broke down after a few miles and had to be abandoned, with their loads going to other rigs. Otherwise, with firm and smooth ice underfoot, Scott found the miles unraveling so quickly that he began to dream of reaching the continent ahead of schedule. Yet he urged his men to an even faster pace. He must take no chances with Amundsen. He needed all the speed he could get.

But speed was not to be his—thanks, oddly enough, to the fact that the weather was good. Though the temperature was well below zero, the air was windless and brilliant with sunlight. The sunlight was the villain. It cheered the troupe, but it cast just enough warmth to soften the snow. So after several days of hard-surface sledging, Scott watched the snow mount higher along the legs of the men and animals with every step they took. Soon the men were floundering up to their waists in the snow. Then it was up to the bellies of the ponies. The dogs could no longer run but had to move forward by leaps and bounds, disappearing one instant below the surface and emerging the next in great explosions of white. It now seemed to Scott that his expedition took as long to travel yards as it had once taken to cover miles.

Throughout November, Scott fought his way across the shelf. Then, on December 5, when he was just twelve miles off the continent, falling snow began to strike his face. At first, it was a lazy snowfall, but it quickly turned into a raging blizzard that drove Scott and his men to their tents for five days. It was the very same storm that halted Amundsen at the summit of the glacier, but it treated Scott far more harshly. Despite the howling winds, the temperature remained mysteriously high, causing the snow that blew into his tents to melt into pools of icy water. His men had no choice but to sit or lie in the pools until the weather cleared.

Scott was on the move again by December 9, coming quickly up to the continent itself. He put into action a plan that he had long held. He left the ponies behind as he moved onto the continent, having intended all the while only to have them help him across the shelf. The supplies on their sledges were stowed aboard other rigs—sledges that would be pulled by the dogs and the men themselves. During his 1902 expedition, Scott had learned that men make excellent sledge teams. They and the dogs would do far better than the ponies could in the slippery, mountainous country ahead.

Once on the continent, Scott started up a broad stretch of ice that rose between the mountains. This was Beardmore Glacier, which for countless centuries had sent tons of ice sliding slowly down to the Ross Shelf. Scott had first sighted it on his 1902 expedition. He felt certain that it ran straight up to the central plateau.

The remainder of December was spent on Beardmore,

and, as far as Scott was concerned, it was a nightmarish month. The snow covering the glacier was as soft as it had been on the shelf. The men sank to their waists in it and fell backward with the weight of their sledges. The dogs disappeared beneath the snow and had to be hauled out bodily. At times, when the dogs could make no foothold in the white softness, the men took them out of the harness, led them up to firmer ground, and then hiked back to fetch their sledges. In such instances, they found themselves walking two miles just to gain one mile of progress.

But the end of the month saw Beardmore behind the group and the central plateau underfoot. In slightly less than two months—without Amundsen's nightmarish maze of valleys and gorges to trouble him—Scott had arrived at 87° south latitude. He was a little more than two hundred miles from the South Pole, and with him now were three sledges and a handful of men. Like Peary in the Arctic, Scott had started out with many sledges and men, planning to return sledges to base camp as soon as the supplies of those sledges became exhausted. With them went the weakest of the men.

Now, here on the plateau, Scott looked at his remaining men. The time was at hand to choose four of their number— the four who would join him in the final run to the South Pole. The men stared back at him out of gaunt and bearded faces, each hoping to be selected. Scott quickly made his choice, pointing to Dr. Edward Wilson, Edgar Evans, Henry Bowers, and Lawrence Oates.

In the main, the quartet was chosen because they were the strongest of the lot. But other considerations played a part in the decision. Wilson, who was thirty-nine years old, had been a member of Scott's 1902 expedition and so, the explorer felt, deserved another chance to reach the South

Pole. Oates, thirty-five, was an army captain; Scott wanted him along to represent the British army in what was primarily a navy expedition. Bowers, twenty-eight, won his berth because of his resistance to the cold, and Evans because he was a giant of a man.

Having made his selection, Scott loaded a single sledge with supplies and, with the foursome serving as a sledge team, headed south on January 4. Calls of good luck came on the wind, and Scott looked back to see the rest of his men waving farewell. Soon they and their two sledges would head back to McMurdo Sound. Every last one of them was disappointed over missing the final push, he knew. But he knew with equal certainty that every last one of them felt deep pride at having come this far.

Then Scott faced south and thrust them from mind. Now he could think of but one man—Amundsen. Was he also on this vast plateau, hurrying toward the South Pole at that very moment?

Once Amundsen achieved the central plateau, he had every reason to believe that good luck was with him again. The weather was clear, the snow underfoot firm, and his men eager to make as much speed as possible. They literally raced their sledges over the flat surface, spinning the miles out behind them. December 13 saw them camp at 89°45′ south latitude, a mere seventeen miles from their goal.

They joked happily among themselves. Seventeen miles! Why that was just a simple little stroll! Nothing could keep them from the South Pole. But Amundsen smiled grimly, for behind their joking he glimpsed worry—the nagging, ever-present worry that Scott might have arrived at the South Pole ahead of them. For days now, while running and while resting, Amundsen's men had constantly squinted off

in all directions, looking for some heart-stopping sign of
Scott—perhaps the dark specks of men moving in the distance, perhaps the slender lines of sledge runners in the
snow.

Fortunately, not a sign of the English explorer had shown
itself to date. Well, Amundsen thought as he settled himself down for the night, tomorrow's march will tell the story.

The next day, under a gray sky, the Norwegians ran their
sledges south. The miles fell away behind them. They peered
all along the horizon, then yelled gleefully to one another,
then peered again. No sign yet—not a trace—that Scott had
preceded them. Still more miles reeled out from under the
sledges, while the yapping of the dogs echoed across the
plateau. Still there was no sign of Scott.

Then, suddenly, the five men were yelling and thumping
each other on the back, the sledges were stopped, and the
dogs were hunkered down in the snow, panting and staring up with bewilderment at the shouting, wildly dancing
explorers. The dogs could not know what the men knew—
that the meters on the sledges now registered the day's run
at seventeen miles. They were at the South Pole, and, for
miles around, not a trace of another expedition was to be
seen.

It was three o'clock in the afternoon, December 14, 1911.
Amundsen had won the race to the South Pole.

The next days were busy ones for the Norwegians. On
December 15, Amundsen sent three of the men out in different directions with instructions to walk for twelve and
one-half miles. He ordered the hike so that, in the event any
of his solar observations had been incorrect, he would be
sure that at least one of his people had crossed the South
Pole. Then, finding that he had indeed made a miscalcula-
tion of eleven miles, Amundsen moved south that distance
and established a new camp, where he erected a small tent

and unfurled the Norwegian flag. He crawled inside the tent and fastened a small plaque to its center pole; inscribed on the plaque were the names of his traveling companions. Then he wrote two notes—one addressed to King Haakon of Norway, the other to Scott. The first informed the king that one of his subjects had reached the South Pole. The second requested Scott to deliver the note to Haakon should a fatal accident overtake the Amundsen party on the return northward.

This work done, Amundsen and his men rested through the night. They smoked cigars that Bjaaland had carried throughout the long journey to celebrate this very occasion. On the morning of December 17, they turned north.

The race was over. Scott, at that time, was still struggling up Beardmore Glacier.

Scott and his companions reached the South Pole on January 17, 1912, only to endure the bitter disappointment of finding Amundsen's tent there, with the plaque and the two notes within. Scott put the notes in his pocket, thanked his men for their efforts, and turned his tired eyes north in proud defeat.

Amundsen reached the Bay of Whales on January 25, 1912, at the end of a northward run so free of difficulty that he called it one of his easiest polar journeys. The entire trip had taken ninety-nine days.

But a different fate awaited Scott's people on the trail north. There they were to write one of the most heroic and tragic pages in the history of polar exploration.

Their troubles began almost as soon as they put the South Pole behind them. Wilson was struck with snow blindness from staring too long without dark glasses into the icy wastes. Scott, while helping to manhandle a sledge over some ice, fell and wrenched a shoulder. Through his pain in

Left to right: Oates, Bowers, Scott, Wilson, and Evans at the South Pole

the next days, Scott saw Evans slowly fall ill with scurvy, the very same illness that had contributed to the defeat of Scott's 1902 expedition. Then, to make matters worse for Evans, the ice collapsed under him and he fell with a cry into a shallow crevasse.

His companions, all of them dizzy with exhaustion, struggled for long minutes to pull him free. Once out, Evans proved too weak to stand, and Scott ordered that he be placed on the sledge, knowing that he was adding an intolerable weight for the men to pull. Evans insisted on walking the next day, but, after several miles, he pitched forward on his face, unconscious. He died that night without again opening his eyes.

Slowly, the party worked its way down from the central plateau to the Ross Ice Shelf, reaching it by March, 1912. By now, all of the travelers looked more like skeletons than men. Their skin was colorless, their cheeks hollow, their eyes puffed almost shut, their movements slow and trembling. Of the lot, Oates was in the poorest condition. His gums were bleeding with scurvy, and his feet were black with frostbite. Though he did not complain once, he shuddered with pain at every step.

Scott knew that every one of the men—himself included —was dangerously close to death. Their only hope was to reach a supply depot that Scott had built on the shelf before heading for the South Pole. There they would find food and medical supplies.

But the Antarctic ruled that Scott was not to reach the depot. A storm whirled across the shelf and halted the men for four days, imprisoning them in their now-ragged tent from March 10–14. The temperature fell to forty degrees below zero. The weather cleared for a few hours on March 14, but the storm returned the next day, and the men crawled back inside the tent. They huddled together for a warmth that could not be had.

In the tent that night, Oates told Scott that he knew he was dying and that he was a terrible burden on his companions. Oates said that he hoped he would die in his sleep. But the dawn found him still alive. He looked at his friends, all of them as sick and haggard as he himself. Painfully, Oates crawled to the tent flap. Worried faces stared after him. He smiled through swollen, peeling lips and spoke calmly: "I'm just going outside and may be some time."

Horrified, the men knew what he had in mind. They raised themselves to stop him. But weak as they were, they could neither move nor speak swiftly enough. Oates crawled through the tent flap and disappeared into the swirling snow, never to be seen again, sacrificing himself to the Antarctic so that his friends might have a better chance to survive.

Scott, deciding that only death awaited in the tent, led his two remaining men out into the storm and, defying its fury, stumbled toward the supply dump. Only there would they find any chance of survival. They struggled on until March 20, at which time they had to stop, unable to see more than a few feet ahead through the falling snow. They were at the time still eleven miles from the supply dump.

The three men, weak to the point of fainting, put up their tent and huddled inside it. They had only a two-day supply of food left. If they were not to die, Scott knew, the storm must break within hours, allowing them to move to the supply dump at once. They had to have food and medical supplies immediately.

But the storm refused to die. It raged on for the rest of the month. The last of the food dwindled away. The tent shuddered and seemed ready to tear itself to shreds in the wind. Scott watched his two friends slowly resign themselves to the idea of death. They wrote final notes to loved ones at home. They talked of suicide for a time but decided that they would wait for whatever fate was in store for them. Suicide was not their way. Besides, hope still sparked now and again. The storm might break at any moment. Somehow, they might find the strength to go on. Scott, his hands trembling, kept a diary of their thoughts.

By March 29, Scott knew that all hope was lost. The storm still howled outside. He took up his diary. Barely able to move his hand, he wrote:

> Every day we have been ready to start for our depot 11 miles away, but outside the door of the tent it remains a scene of whirling drifts. I do not think that we can hope for any better things now. We shall stick it out to the end, but we are getting weaker, of course, and the end cannot be far.
>
> It seems a pity, but I do not think I can write more.
>
> R. Scott

Then, almost as an afterthought, he added another sentence: "For God's sake, look after our people."

Scott wrote no more.

Back at McMurdo Sound, the men of Scott's expedition decided to launch a search for the explorer in the next weeks. It was not until November, however, that they found the little tent buried in ice and snow in the vast expanse of the Ross Ice Shelf. Scott's diary and the letters written home by the doomed trio were brought back to civilization, but the bodies of the three men were left in the ice to which they had given their lives. The tent was draped about them and a cairn of rocks was built over them, to stand there in icy loneliness to this day. The tragedy was done.

A Final Note

A ND NOW, AT LAST, we have come to our own time, having traveled the long road of adventure, daring, and accomplishment from the moment when man became a hunter at the dawn of time to the twentieth century—our century, an era of strange contrasts.

On the one hand, it has been the century of two world wars and a seemingly endless chain of smaller conflicts. It has been the century of the nuclear weapon, of air and water pollution, of overcrowded, restless cities.

But, on the other hand, it has been a century of magnificent accomplishments—the airplane, the rocket, radio and television, the automobile, radar, the laser beam. We have developed new tools for the fight against disease and new ideas for the fight against ignorance and poverty and superstition.

Ours is also the century of great explorations. We can thank the scientific and technological accomplishments for many of those explorations.

First, there is the airplane. With it, we are now within hours of the world's most remote regions, regions that the explorers of earlier times could not reach in weeks or months —if, indeed, they could reach them at all. With the airplane, we are able to bring supplies and aid swiftly to expeditions working their way through the wilds. With it, Admiral Richard E. Byrd was able to fly over the North Pole in 1926 and then over the South Pole three years later.

Next, there is the submarine. Australia's Sir George Hubert Wilkins first put it to use in exploration when, in 1931, he submerged his *Nautilus* off Spitzbergen and attempted to sail beneath the Arctic Ocean ice to the North Pole. Heavy storms and mechanical difficulties turned him back far short of his goal, but nuclear submarines of the U.S. Navy—the *Nautilus,* the *Skate,* and the *Seadragon*—in the late 1950s completed the work that Wilkins had started. Throughout the world, the submarine, in a variety of forms and sizes is enabling today's oceanographers to study the geology and life forms deep below the surface of our seas.

Then there is the automobile—and its sturdier brothers, the truck and the tractor. The automobile and truck were invaluable as personnel- and cargo-carriers when America's Roy Chapman Andrews explored the great Gobi Desert in the 1920s. The tractor performed the same service for England's Sir Vivian Fuchs when, between November 24, 1957, and March 2, 1958, he made man's first transcontinental crossing of Antarctica, a journey of 2,158 miles that took him across the South Pole from the Weddell Sea on the Atlantic side of the continent to McMurdo Sound on the Pacific side. Today, all three vehicles are being used wherever man is exploring.

Exploration in this century has been helped not only by scientific and technological developments but by the ability of explorers, scientists, scholars, and technicians of all nationalities to cooperate with one another.

The most striking example of this cooperation was seen during the International Geophysical Year. Actually a period of eighteen months—from July, 1957, to December, 1958—the International Geophysical Year saw the men of some seventy nations establish two thousand stations across the world for the purpose of studying the nature of our planet and its atmosphere. Together, they searched beneath the sea, explored and mapped the least known of our land areas, nosed out and investigated new natural resources, and tuned in on the behavior of the atmosphere with countless meteorological and astronomical instruments.

More than 15 million records of the earth, the sea, and the sky were made during this period. The records are still under study at universities and in laboratories across the world. As each study is completed, it is distributed to the men of all the participating countries.

It is our ability to move through the air, however, that has made possible the most striking explorations of this century—or of any other century, for that matter. With this ability, we have not only broken free of the ground but have blasted out of our atmospheric shell and have entered that most mysterious and challenging of all regions—outer space.

Space exploration began late in the last century with the handful of scientists who began to tinker with the rocket, the engine that, because it does not require outside oxygen to operate, can carry us beyond the earth's atmosphere. The development of the rocket continued into this century until, in the late 1950s, Russia put the famed *Sputnik* into orbit. The development of space exploration gathered momentum, and the next years saw America's first suborbital flights, followed by the orbital missions of such men as Russia's Yuri Gagarin and America's John Glenn, Scott Carpenter, and Virgil Grissom.

The goal of all these breathtaking flights—and of the many unmanned space shots—was to prepare us for our first journey to another planet, an age-old goal that was realized in 1969 when Astronaut Neil Armstrong stepped down to the gray dust of the moon's surface and remarked: "That's one small step for man—one giant leap for mankind."

Those words will live in the pages of history for as long as there is a history. To all, they must rank among the most memorable words ever spoken.

But to man, knowing that his kind is ever on the move and ever curious about the unknown, Armstrong's statement must also pose a question—the question that has been asked at the close of every successful exploration since the beginning of time. Where will we go next?